Dedication

This book is dedicated to the people who use their leadership influence to make a positive difference in the personal and professional lives of everyone they meet.

To the organizations that strive each day to live out the values that result in a healthy workplace environment that produces inspired performance at all levels.

In honor of my wife, who unknowingly challenges me every day to be a better man. And to our children Laura Lee and Jake who give me a never ending supply of joy and motivation.

Culturetopia

The ultimate
high-performance
workplace

Shiela,
I wish you a fond Aloha!

by Jason Young

BetterWay Publishing
Dallas, Texas

Published in the United States by:
BetterWay Publishing
P.O. Box 118046
Carrollton, TX 75011
info@betterwaypublishing.com
www.betterwaypublishing.com

First Edition

ISBN 978-1-60530-668-1

Printed in the United States of America

Table of Contents

Introduction

What makes companies productive and profitable? Look around the business and management section in your local bookstore and you'll find plenty of books on this topic. There seem to be lots of different answers. Depending on which book you read, the secret lies in process re-engineering, effective teamwork, motivation, project management, organization, goal-setting … and the list goes on.

What makes people happy and fulfilled? Look around the psychology and self-help sections in your local bookstore and you'll find plenty of books on this topic, too. There seem to be lots of different answers. Depending on which book you read, the answer lies in self-understanding, therapy, religion, selfishness, selflessness, helping others, meditation, exercise, diet … and the list goes on.

This book, *Culturetopia*, is my contribution to both discussions. What I have found in my years as an employee, trainer, manager, and consultant is that these two questions have a lot of answers in common. In short, many of the actions a company can take to improve productivity are actions that also make employees happier and more fulfilled. And vice versa: the actions a company takes to create a satisfying work environment result in improved productivity.

Successful companies are successful, largely because employees do good work.

And it turns out that people do their best work in a corporate culture that allows them to make a useful contribution, gives them some control over their working lives, and respects them as human beings.

The key to employee fulfillment and to employee productivity is the company's culture.

Most adults spend around half their waking lives at work, and many of them would rather be doing something else. If a person is going to spend that much time in any one endeavor, then they ought to enjoy it. Unfortunately, many corporate executives believe that most employees are there just trading hours for dollars, so they constantly strive to motivate and cajole or pressure people to perform better to produce more profits for the company. Some companies still operate in a cultural environment in which there is a constant tension between *workers* and *managers*. *Managers assume workers* want to do as little work as possible for as much pay as possible. Workers assume managers are solely focused on extracting as much production as possible for as small a cost as possible.

In *Culturetopia*, I describe the path to a better way, where employees are naturally inspired to produce their best work, and where managers spend most of their time helping them to do exactly that.

Entrepreneurs and business managers who understand the cultural factors that lead to success will be equipped to create an organizational culture where employees can do their best work and one that will produce the desired performance improvements in the areas of productivity, profitability, employee retention, and customer satisfaction.

In this book, I discuss management decisions and actions from the perspective of *shaping the culture*. This means creating a working environment in which all employees can be fully engaged in performing satisfying, productive work. Working in a company with a high-performance culture really is more enjoyable for employees than working in a low-performance culture. That doesn't mean it's an easy option for anyone.

Creating the right culture needs a sustained management effort, clear and unsentimental thinking, and tough decisions. The end result will be: higher levels of employee performance, contribution, and productivity; greater customer satisfaction; and a financially successful business. At the same time, this highly productive environment will result in satisfied and fulfilled employees and a much less stressful workplace, even a joyful workplace, for everyone.

1

Welcome to Culturetopia

Right from the start, you know this is going to be a different place to work. Jackie, at the front desk, is warm and friendly; not phony friendliness, but the real warmth you find when a genuinely sociable person is doing work that she loves, and that she's good at. She is expecting you, knows why you're there, and is able to answer all your questions. She has your welcome packet ready and makes sure you're scheduled for the next new employee orientation, the *New Hire Celebration*. She doesn't have to look up everything on a screen or in a binder; she just has it there in her head, because she's obviously interested. You ask her how the company stock was performing and, yes, she knows all about that, too. OK, that was an unfair test, but she passes anyway.

This is a company that's obviously doing well, and has been for some time. It has nicely laid out space and interesting, but not ostentatious, decor. There's a friendly atmosphere and you feel comfortable already.

Your first meeting is with your new boss, Julie.

Two hours later, you feel even better about winning this job. People were lining up for this opportunity. On paper, maybe it's not the highest paid job you could go for, but you're starting to feel confident that you'll be better off here than anywhere else in town.

Julie has given you a complete briefing on the company: its products, customers, the way it does business, and where it's going. You've been introduced to everyone else in the department. They're a very diverse group of people: men and women, all ages, a variety of ethnicities. But they *all share something* that's not easy to pin down right away.

Two days later, it's becoming clearer. You've never had so much help in a new job before. People are enthusiastic about working with you and are doing everything they can to help you be successful. Everyone knows what they are supposed to do in their jobs and gladly share that information. They're able to tell you what the company expects you to do as well. You quickly feel a part of the team: a *knowledgeable and expert team.*

You have just one concern, and it's a big one. This company seems to have extremely high expectations and they want you to deliver high-quality work and lots of it.

You're an experienced person, yet you're not sure how it can all be done.

Two weeks go by and you realize with some surprise that it's still going really well. Everyone is still positive and supportive. You haven't come across any of the petty jealousies, office politics, or angry arguments that were commonplace at your previous job. Sure, there have been plenty of discussions about the work, about the best way to do things. But somehow, and you're not sure how this happens, people just talk it through, then come to a rational decision, and things work out fine. These conflicts are addressed quickly and they seem to increase respect and productivity by providing an outlet for frustration.

You also realize that you're getting through a ton of work every day. In your last job, you stayed late at work most nights. You took work home on weekends just so you didn't fall behind and look incompetent. Here, you do everything that's expected of you and you still get home to spend some time with the kids. You find you have more time to think and you've already come up with some great ideas on how to improve the work. Well, you thought all your ideas were great. At least one of them was: the team just implemented the change right away.

Another bright idea was maybe not so smart: a team member pointed out the one key factor you had over-looked and explained why that one was important. But it all led to you understanding the work even better, and that feels good.

Two months later. You've become used to the idea that your experience as a new employee wasn't just some kind of beginner's luck. This is the way this place operates all the time, for everyone. It's highly productive, highly efficient, and an immensely satisfying place to work. Sure, you've enjoyed work before, in other companies, but you realize that the work itself wasn't much fun: some of the people you worked with made it bearable. Here, the work is fun *and* the people are great.

One year later. You're really happy in your job. You've learned a lot and some of the work that you struggled with for a while you can now handle with ease, thanks to coaching from your boss and colleagues, and a couple of outside training courses. Sure, you've made some mistakes, including one major blunder. The first time you slipped up (something quite trivial), you reacted in a pretty normal way. At first, you felt embarrassed, not wanting to let your colleagues know; but the working atmosphere was so comfortable, you took a deep breath, accepted responsibility, and asked for help. *Help* is exactly what you got; no blame, no criticism, no snide comments. You soon found that if you accepted responsibility, then others would support you. No one wasted time and energy on blame and recrimination. So when your time came to really mess up (it happens to all of us), you were all set to seek help, confident that the team would rally around you, which is exactly what happened.

Three years later. Your job has evolved into something slightly different now. You've taken on some new work, tasks you particularly enjoy doing and do well, and other people have taken over some of the tasks in areas where you weren't so productive.

You like this. There are always new things to learn, and there are always new challenges to be faced, but at the same time, you've come to feel tremendously capable. You know that there will always be opportunities for taking on more responsibilities in this company, if that is what you want. You get things done. You feel that you are a part of something bigger, something that matters. You're making a difference.

Over the years, you've gained an understanding of how this company is special and different from any other company you've worked for. You understand how it can be relaxed and highly productive at the same time, how it can deliver great value for customers and still make good profits, how the approach to the job can be seriously professional, and also be enjoyable.

You realize that there isn't one unique thing that makes the company special. It's everything: the attitude of each employee towards his or her work; the constant concern to make customers happy; the way people work together in teams; that ever-present mix of fun, hard work, high standards, and learning new things every day; the generous way each one of your co-workers helps you to do a better job when you need support — and then lets you get on with it when you're doing fine.

You've found that, in this environment, your co-workers quickly become your friends. Your attitude to the work and to your customers has become consistently positive. You like to get out of bed in the morning and go to work, and you have a great sense of satisfaction on your way home in the evening. It's nice to have close friends at work, especially in the winter, when it's cold and dark and you need that extra motivation to get going.

It's your five-year anniversary. You're still happy to be a part of this company. Maybe a couple more years, another promotion or two, and you might start to look around for something elsewhere, but there's a problem: where can you find another company like this one?

Maybe you'll have to start a company of your own.

2
Company Culture

All right, the company I just described may not actually exist, but if it did, wouldn't you want to work there? I call this kind of idealized, highly productive working environment *Culturetopia*.

Culturetopia is a culture of care and accountability. This kind of culture recognizes that company success is delivered by the people who work in that company, so it makes sense to care for the needs of those people and, at the same time, hold them accountable for results. This is the kind of culture where employees get to do work they enjoy and find satisfying, with people they like and respect. This is the kind of culture that makes it natural for people to want to make a contribution and feel empowered to do so. They bring their full talents to the workplace and they work hard. They derive high levels of satisfaction from their accomplishments. This all leads to a positive, upward spiral of performance improvement.

Culturetopia is an ideal to aspire to.

Most people who work for companies work in a more traditional *command and control* environment, a pre-Culturetopian environment. But Culturetopia is not just a theoretical notion. It's real. In fact, many companies have some of the cultural attributes I described. It's just highly unusual to experience them all in one place.

At this stage, you might be wondering exactly what I mean by company culture. I'll explain.

* * *

We often use the word *culture* when we are talking about groups of people. We talk about national cultures and also about the culture of a neighborhood within a city. Individual tribes, ethnic groups, and entire nations all have their own special cultures. Clubs, families, religions, and workplaces have their own cultures, and it is possible for one person to participate in more than one culture at a time.

Any group of people who come into contact with each other in their daily lives to work, play, or socialize will eventually develop a group culture.

The culture of a group is reflected in the way that the people in that group act and behave. Their behavior is influenced by their traditions, assumptions, values, and beliefs.

People who share a culture have similar attitudes
towards life and similar perspectives on the world around
them, while retaining their identity as individuals. This
individuality means that, while people don't necessarily act
or respond in exactly the same way as each other, they are
likely to act in ways consistent with the common aims and
common values of the shared culture.

Mostly, cultures seem to simply emerge and evolve.
No one sat down to purposefully design and build the
culture of the Masai in East Africa, or the culture of the
Inuit in Arctic Canada, or the culture of the mid-west
farming communities in the United States, but they all
indisputably have cultures. The culture within an individual family is not contained in some sort of blueprint.
There is no documented master plan that pre-determines
the culture of social sub-groups: each individual golf
club, book club, church, online gaming community, and
neighborhood bar develops its own distinctive character,
its own culture. No single person invented the culture of
the music-loving party crowd in downtown Austin, or the
culture of the reading group that meets in a restaurant in
downtown Boston.

It's obvious that most cultures don't evolve in
accordance with a pre-defined plan. It's equally clear that
cultures are created by people, and that some people in

each group have more influence on the direction of cultural growth than others. These influencers are the people I call Cultural Leaders; and they don't necessarily have to be the officially appointed leaders in the community or group to wield influence.

* * *

Like any other group of connected people, each business organization has its own culture. Every company, large or small, has a culture: if you put people together in any organization for some time, a culture will start to form.

We can tell a lot about the underlying culture by the way people behave. Behavior is influenced by our feelings, values, beliefs, ambitions, training, and knowledge. Behavior is also affected by how much we like and respect the people we're working with and working for. Also, it's influenced by our attitude to the work itself: whether we see it as an important contribution to our lives and the lives of others, or as something we'd rather not be doing.

All of these factors go together in a single concept: company culture.

* * *

If you have worked in a business environment for just a few years, you will have observed, as I have, some of the cultural realities of successful businesses. You don't need to be a consultant or a corporate trouble-shooter to appreciate that:

- Companies that treat their customers in a fair and friendly manner get repeat business and earn more revenues. The way that people handle customers depends on their own attitudes and assumptions, and also on the values and policies of the company: company culture.

- Effective teamwork leads to more innovation and higher productivity. What drives effective teamwork and productive collaboration? Largely, it's determined by the attitude of team members towards each other and their motivation to do good work together: again, company culture.

- When employees know what is expected of them, have the right tools, and are properly trained to do their jobs, they produce better results than if they are expected to work things out as they go along: company culture.

- Rewarding productive behavior leads to more productive behavior. Punishing people for lack of productivity never results in a world-class workforce: again, company culture.

- Companies that give their employees opportunities to contribute, to learn and grow, find that employees generally seize these opportunities, take responsibility, and become more productive as a result. Once again, this is an aspect of company culture.

* * *

If the most important factor influencing employee behavior is company culture, then what decides company culture? Who makes it? Where does it come from?

Culture evolves in a complicated and iterative way, with the actions and attitudes of everyone in the company having a complex interactive effect on everyone else. Everyone's behavior is affected in some way by the pre-existing company culture and, at the same time, everyone's behavior helps to determine the evolution path of the culture.

If managers don't recognize the role they play in developing the culture, then they will act in ways that may drive the culture in an unhelpful direction. They may also allow behaviors of others to dominate the environment.

In other words, if company executives, managers, and supervisors do not work together to create the type of culture that leads to high performance, then some other type of culture will emerge, and the chances are it will not be a high-performance culture in which people throughout the company can do their best work.

The culture of a company depends critically on *corporate lifestyle* decisions. Culture starts at the top of the corporation, department, branch, or team. Management decisions and actions will influence the development of company culture for better or worse. So, if anything is going to change for the better, then managers must accept responsibility for identifying the need and for making it happen. Smart business managers aim to create a culture to which everyone can feel they *belong*. If managers live in one world and all the workers are in a different world, then the company will never be successful.

It follows that executives, managers, and supervisors must take deliberate and thoughtful steps to mold the culture through their behavior, decisions, and attitudes.

This affects all aspects of company life: recruitment,

selection, training, coaching, management style, policies, procedures, role definitions, and more.

It is the job of the decision makers, managers, and supervisors in the company to *lead smart*. Smart corporate leaders understand the importance of culture and know that the formation and evolution of culture should not simply be left to chance. They purposefully strive to create an environment where employees can do their best work and where everyone can be a contributor.

3
Dangerous Assumptions

People make assumptions and those assumptions guide their thinking, behavior, and decisions. Some assumptions reflect reality. Some assumptions are wholly wrong, and are quickly discovered to be so by rational people. Other assumptions are just partly wrong or are wrong in a way that is not readily obvious.

People make assumptions about company culture. Some of these assumptions can drive a company in the wrong cultural direction, away from Culturetopia. Three important dangerous assumptions are:

- Company culture doesn't matter that much.
- Managers are in charge.
- Cultural alignment just happens.

Dangerous Assumption #1: Culture Doesn't Matter that Much

It's comforting for some people to think of business organizations as machines: if they're well-designed and well-oiled, they should work. It's true that companies need processes, procedures, rules, computer systems, structure, and organization; and sometimes there is a strong similarity between a company's operations and a piece of machinery. But organizations contain something that is not inside any machine: people. People have their own individual thoughts, ideals, preferences, and dreams. People together create cultures.

I see similarities between the workplace and the family. Early childhood behavior is heavily influenced by the culture of the family. The family culture is reflected in the behavior of other family members: parents especially, but also brothers, sisters, grandparents, and others. Later, children are influenced by friends, coaches, teachers, and others at school, in the playground, and in the neighborhood. Children learn behavioral patterns early, and many of those behaviors are linked to the influences of others. It's not so much that you have good children or bad children, more that you have children whose behavior is good, or whose behavior is bad. The environment they've grown up in *molds* their behavior. Good behavior and bad behavior can equally be corrected or reinforced by the actions and reactions of others.

Eventually, children grow up and, as adults, most of them go to work. They come with pre-existing attitudes and behavior patterns, but they're still not fully formed. There are still plenty of opportunities for people in the workplace (executives, managers, supervisors, and front-line employees) to influence behaviors through instruction or example.

Consequently, I believe, and there's evidence to back me up, that the number one factor influencing the behavior of employees of any company is the environment in which they work: the company culture.

If the culture is unhealthy, employees do not strive for the benefit of their customers or for their company, or even for themselves. There are no good or bad employees, just good or bad employee behavior; and behavior is influenced, more than anything else, by company culture. Culture matters.

Dangerous Assumption #2: Managers are in Charge

Managers generally believe that employee behavior is driven more or less directly by management decisions and policies. This way of looking at the corporate world suggests that, if the business doesn't succeed, then either managers made the wrong decisions or the employees simply didn't do what they were asked (or instructed) to do.

But who actually runs your company? Think before answering. If you are a manager that has experienced difficulty making changes in your company, then maybe you aren't in charge after all.

Have you ever worked in a company where the management team came up with a great plan but, somehow, it just didn't seem to work out as you envisioned it? Some managers become perplexed because of their inability to make things happen just the way they want them. The fact is that, no matter what decisions are made by managers, people will generally do what they prefer to do.

Employee behavior is determined not just by what the bosses tell employees to do, but also by what the employees themselves want to do.

Sometimes management plans do not achieve the desired results because the employees who are expected to make the plans work have different ideas of what they should do. This is not necessarily conscious obstructionism, nor is it simply a failure to communicate. It happens because people are working on different assumptions, on different wavelengths. They belong to different cultures.

The psychologist Jonathan Haidt describes the

relationship between the human conscious mind and the subconscious mind as a *rider on an elephant.* Often, what a person's conscious mind wants to do is overruled by the subconscious, which sometimes takes the person in surprising and unpredictable directions.

This analogy applies to companies, too. In a company, the CEO and the board might make a purposeful decision and announce it with all the energy and enthusiasm they can muster, but the corporate elephant will continue on whatever path it wants to take, and there's not much the rider (the little person sitting on top) can do about it.

So, the management team in a company is just a rider on an elephant, and if the elephant wants to eat over *there*, not over *here*, then that's what the elephant will do, even if it does it quietly while the management's mind is busy on something else.

There may not be active resistance to change, it's just that the changes won't happen, or they won't happen in quite the way you planned. If there is cultural misalignment, the aims, preferences, and assumptions of some people in the company will be completely different from the aims, preferences, and assumptions of others.

> What happens, or doesn't happen, in an organization depends on who wields the power to do things differently, not who issues the orders.

In many cases, managers are working against the embedded culture of a company, trying to initiate changes that are unwanted, or considered unnecessary by the people who actually have to change. Sometimes managers can come up with horribly wrong ideas, and cultural inertia can minimize the damage. Sometimes managers are exactly right to want to initiate changes that will benefit the company, but cultural inertia gets in the way.

When managers work *against* culture like this, they become frustrated and even angry at their inability to achieve the results they're aiming for. Anger and frustration do not help: these emotions just get in the way. Anger drives managers to try to get people to do something close to what they want by forcing them, or by making it difficult or stressful to do something else. This is a *command and control* culture. Extreme forms of command and control assume that managers are all wise and knowledgeable and workers are dumb and compliant. But none of this is necessary or desirable if we understand how to build a culture that works *for everyone*, that aligns

what people want from their working lives with what
owners and managers want for their company.

Suppose the people in the company overwhelmingly
are in tune with management decisions and want the same
things for the company as the management team does.
That is, they want company success and the opportunity
to share in that success, and they want the satisfaction
derived from working usefully and productively towards
common goals. What kind of a difference would that
culture make? It would lead to more cohesion, less
conflict, more success, and more satisfaction all around.
The elephant and the rider work together as a team. This
is *cultural alignment*.

To get cultural factors on your side, you need to
shape the culture to align with the aims, aspirations, and
needs of the people who actually *do the real work* (the
frontline employees) and with the needs of the company
for business success. Working *with* company culture
ensures that employee behavior will deliver business
results, without micro management, without arguments,
and without coercion.

Cultural alignment moves us from a command and
control environment in which managers believe they are
the primary agents of constructive change and perfect

performance, into a collaborative culture in which **every-one** really is an agent of change and a contributor to the excellent performance of the company. Cultural alignment moves us closer to Culturetopia.

Dangerous Assumption #3: Cultural Alignment Just Happens

Cultural alignment is when everyone in a company buys in to the same broad set of cultural values and agreed behaviors.

For their part, the frontline employees (*frontliners*) need to be in tune with company values, realizing that they have a responsibility to themselves, to each other, and to the company, to develop their own abilities to produce their best work.

This is not about the workers being brainwashed into accepting what management has to say: that would seriously miss the point; the result would not be Culturetopia, just a different type of command and control. A company of obedient clones might appear to work well for a time, but it will not be open to change and the contribution of everyone will be severely limited.

True, Culturetopia needs frontline employees to buy in to Culturetopian values. But the real benefit starts to build when managers and executives buy in to the values, too — for example, by understanding that everyone can make a creative contribution, and everyone can exert influence to improve company performance.

When everyone in a company is aligned with the same set of values, they become *free to contribute* by putting forward their best ideas, and doing their best work.

Cultural alignment has to be planned, created, nurtured, and maintained.

When the culture of a company is not the focus of anyone's attention, it's easy to assume that the right culture will just happen: put in place the right business processes, train the people to do a great job, and success will follow. Is it really that easy to build a high-performance company?

In fact, building a truly productive cultural environment is not easy, or everyone would already be doing it. It is especially difficult if you're starting from a position of severe misalignment; it's much easier if you're starting with a small group of like-minded people in a new enterprise. Successful companies have discovered that it is worth the effort, because once a degree of cultural alignment is in place, everything becomes easier and more productive.

The process of alignment should start (ideally) at the company's inception. Any new company's entrepreneurial founders, if they are smart, ask themselves the question: *What are we trying to achieve here?*

At the same time, they should also ask themselves: *What are the values this company must have to ensure that everyone works together to achieve our goals?*

These two questions must be asked and answered together. In the inevitable excitement and rush to get a new company going, questions about the culture are often asked much later. It's a bit like building a new office complex and, some time later, asking the question: *Did anyone remember to install the plumbing?*

If you find yourself in a company that hasn't thought much about its culture before, you may discover some surprises (good surprises and bad surprises) when you start to examine the type of culture in which you find yourself. But taking an honest look at the current culture is essential.

* * *

The next step is to ensure that people in all positions in the company are broadly in tune with the stated values. This means recruiting people who are broadly sympathetic to the attitudes and aims that prevail within the company, and that you want to continue. Candidate sourcing and selection, therefore, involves weighing factors of attitude and personality alongside specific technical and intellectual skills. Does the human resources department emphasize the company's cultural values in its recruiting practices? Do the recruiters in your company understand what types of cultures exist in different departments and the impact those cultures will have on new employees? Do they know how to select people who will *perform well* in those cultures? (We are looking for performance, not conformance. We want people to bloom in our culture, not simply to survive.)

Joining a new company is like joining a new tribe. Even if you know the language, you need to learn the customs. The company must help each employee learn the values and the employee must want to learn.

The learning process starts on day one, and the reinforcement of values has to happen all day, every day. The way people collaborate, the reward systems, the role of managers (mentors), and the physical environment of the company: all of these, and more, play a part in build-ing understanding of the common values and company culture.

Embedding common values requires great effort.

Achieving cultural wellness is not a one-off project. It requires a continuing effort and must result in a lasting change in many facets of the way the company goes about its work: the values, policies, rules, and guidelines that people apply every day; the way it sources and recruits people; how it inducts them into the company; how it trains and coaches them; how it ensures that people know what is expected of them; the way it rewards, encourages, and enthuses everyone in the company; and more.

It is even more difficult for a company to change its way of life than it is for a single human being. The decision to eat more steamed vegetables and less fried chicken is difficult enough for one person to make and stick to. When a company decides to change its process for handling customer problems, many different people have to understand the changes, be committed to them, and make them work.

Whether you're trying to stick to a diet, or stick to Culturetopian values, I realize that, at first, it seems easier just to keep doing the same thing as yesterday.

Culturetopia won't just happen by itself. It's hard work.

That's why I have developed assessments, work-

books and training materials that focus on specific aspects
of achieving a high performance workplace culture.

Cultural alignment starts with values, and so the
remainder of this book will focus there: on the values that
are important in creating a high-performance company
culture, on the values that are the foundation for
Culturetopia.

Business executives, managers, and supervisors have
an ongoing duty to build cultural alignment: shaping the
culture goes with the job. In fact, shaping the culture *is*
the job! Welcome to a lot of responsibility.

4

Culturetopia
Versus
Traditional Management

The starting point is where we are, and most of us
are embedded in companies that have few, if any, of the
positive attributes of Culturetopia. Most companies still
rely on a number of assumptions: that managers should
understand what everyone in the company is supposed to
do, that managers are smart enough to get everyone to do
what they are told, and that good employees are those
who do what managers tell them to do.

These assumptions are typical of most *command-and-
control-style* pre-Culturetopian companies. The problem is
not that these assumptions about management and
employees are always completely wrong, just that they're
never completely right. The assumptions contain enough
truth to convince lots of people to keep assuming them,
but these assumptions aren't solid enough to provide the
foundation for a successful, high-performing business.

Traditionally managed companies have a fundamental weakness: everyone is pulling hard, but in different directions and for different reasons.

What is the impact of the command-and-control approach of traditional management? Choose a large corporation at random and ask a few people who work there a few simple questions. The answers will show just how far away the organization is from Culturetopia.

In a low-productivity culture here are some of the replies you might get:

How productive are you at work? Well, I guess I personally get a lot of work done every day, but I waste so much time on other stuff.

Such as? Attending useless meetings. Arguing my position. Protecting myself from company politics. Doing stuff to impress my boss. Above all, firefighting: I can't seem to get much work done without having to handle some kind of problem or crisis.

Is this just you, or is everyone like that? Pretty much everyone. Some people seem to have found a way to keep out of all those side issues, but they're not the ones who call the shots. And they're not going to get promoted, either.

How good is your company at finding new ideas for doing things better? Not good. For a start, most of us who know enough about the way things are done around here don't have much time to sit back and think. And if one of us does suggest something new, it's an uphill struggle to get anything changed.

What's the general atmosphere like at work? Our group is pretty good: we have good people. We help each other out sometimes but mostly we try to get our own work done as best we can. Some people in other groups are downright hostile. Personally, I try to keep out of their way. Other people just love to complain about everything. That wastes a lot of time, every day.

What sort of stuff do they complain about? Everything. Who gets to do what work. Decisions being made about the job and the way we do things. Most are complaining about how *they* are pinning the blame on *us* or someone else is at fault when something goes wrong. You know, CYA.

What are the opportunities like for promotion? Now that's one good thing about the company. We lose a lot of people every year, so there are plenty of chances for promotion. In fact, for some people, angling for promotion is just about the main thing they spend time on. It's a bit of a rat race.

Doesn't that mean a lot of supervisors and managers are quite inexperienced? Oh, yes. I guess that could be a problem, but it doesn't seem to worry anyone much. It doesn't worry me: it means that when I get a promotion, no one will notice that I don't know much.

Why is your company in business? Well, to make stuff, sell it at a profit. I guess it's to make the owners and top bosses rich and happy.

Are they rich and happy? Well, they're certainly not happy, given how much they push us to save money. So I suppose they must feel they're not rich enough yet.

How about you and the other employees? Are you rich? Are you happy? Are you kidding? I'd leave tomorrow if I didn't need the paycheck.

* * *

As we move forward towards Culturetopia, we may have to change some job titles, too. Traditional job titles in traditional companies don't help us much. In Culturetopia, we may eventually have to make some logical changes.

In Culturetopia, who manages work? Everyone does, so in Culturetopia everyone is a manager. Who supervises? Everyone. Who are the leaders? Everyone.

Since these terms apply to everyone in Culturetopia, they are no longer useful. So we might have some fun and change job titles around just to remind ourselves who really does what.

Let's start with the people who directly drive the customer experience. Those are the employees who make products for customers or provide services for customers, whether they are in direct contact with customers or not. By customers, we mean external (paying) customers and also internal customers within the business. This large group includes the customer service reps, production line operators, field sales reps, technicians, crafts specialists, the office workers in accounts, procurement, human resources, and many others. The daily efforts of these workers create results for customers. They are the people who **do** things, who **execute** on the frontline. Collectively, maybe they should be called doers, or even executives. I prefer to call them *frontliners.*

There is a second group of workers who have a different role, also valuable in its own way. This next group selects the right people for the workforce and puts in place the right training, coaching, tools, and logistics support. They design and optimize processes and set standards for performance and behavior. This group is there to help the frontliners deliver their best work. They assist and support and guide those on the frontline and keep an eye on performance and behavior. Is there one word that covers all of that? Yes, but it isn't *manager* and it isn't *supervisor*. There is a better term: *mentor.*

The title *mentor* comes from the story of Ulysses and the Trojan war. As Ulysses joins the Greeks to bring back Helen from far-off Troy, he is worried about leaving his son, Telemachus. So Ulysses appoints a trusted and experienced friend whose name was Mentor to guide and instruct his son while he is away. Mentor took the job seriously, stating: "I will go to Ithaca, to put heart into Ulysses' son Telemachus; I will embolden him."

Mentoring is more than just coaching: it encompasses guidance, support, instruction, commitment and direction. In other words, mentors supply what the frontliners need to consistently do their best work.

At some higher levels of the organization, a third group of people is somewhat detached from the day-to-day activities of business operations. The role such employees play is primarily to provide broad direction and set the course for the company. They find investors, decide where the company should be going, what it needs to do to get there, and plan the route. Traditional companies place these managers in the ranks of company executives, or chiefs — C-levels and their support teams. We could logically call them navigators, but let's (for once) stick to current acceptable terminology and call them *chiefs*.

So, a Culturetopian company might, with logic on its side, call frontline employees *frontliners*; supervisors and mid-managers *mentors*; and those on the executive team *chiefs*.

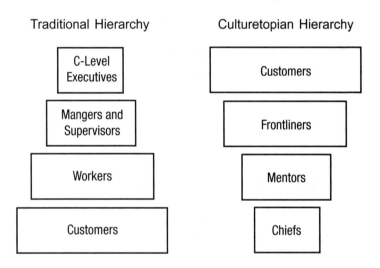

5
In Culturetopia,
Values are Central

The values defined by and espoused by the founders and the owners of the company provide the central themes that drive everything else. Values guide attitudes. Attitudes influence behavior and behavior produces outcomes. The outcomes of having Culturetopian values include: high productivity, high customer satisfaction and high employee loyalty.

Every company has values. It's not enough just to have values, because values can drive companies towards mediocrity and failure, just as they can drive them in good and profitable directions.

It's important that the values should be the *right type of values*.

Culturetopian companies have Culturetopian values.

The way values are regarded by the company and its employees is also important. Culturetopian companies take their values seriously.

Built-in Values

In Culturetopia, values are built into the company's way of doing business.

In Culturetopia, values are actually used every day to guide every employee's workplace behavior. Whenever an employee is in doubt about what to do next in any situation, then the company's values can provide guidance.

In a company that aspires to become successful by building a culture of cooperation, values provide an *attitude ecosystem* that works to guide employee behavior in every job, every moment of the working day.

In some pre-Culturetopian companies, values are merely words on a poster; or a couple of sentences in the introductory blurb to the annual report, a blurb that most readers skip. This is management's way of telling people what to think and feel, and it usually doesn't work. If employees know what the values of the company are, it's likely because their boss has told them to commit the words to memory. They could pass a test by reciting the text, but it makes no difference to their everyday working lives.

In a Culturetopian business, values are a reflection of what everyone in the company believes. Everyone knows the values, because they identify with them. People are therefore aligned with the values because those values are *their* values, not because someone else has told them what to believe.

The values work alongside the mission to create an environment that influences every action by every employee. Moreover, the values are consistently applied to everyone involved in or impacted by the business of the company: employees, customers, stakeholders, and the community at large.

There are two ways in which the world gets to know about the values of a company:

- **Expressed values:** These are formal statements made by the company to its employees, its customers, its shareholders, and to the world at large.

- **Implicit values:** These values are implied by the way a company behaves.

While a company's board members might assume that their values are the formal statements over which they deliberate every few years, the world pays much more attention to how the company actually behaves.

For example, a car dealership might have a beautifully framed mission statement on the wall declaring that their salespeople will help customers to buy the most suitable car for their needs, and do it by providing friendly, helpful, and honest advice. The same car dealership could set commission levels that encourage salespeople to always sell the most profitable models, no matter what the customers' real needs are. Which values will determine the salesperson's behavior, the values expressed in the statement hanging on the wall or the implicit values contained in the commission rates? What are the true values of a company that does this? No argument: it's what the company does, not what it says, that counts and people inside the company who think differently are kidding themselves.

If a company tells the world that it is always open and honest with shareholders, and yet it concocts financial results that are deliberately misleading, which is the true expression of its values? Of course: it's how the company acts, not how it *says* it will act, that matters.

If I tell everyone I'm on a low-fat diet and every few days I secretly treat myself to a bucket of fried chicken, am I actually on a diet or not? Not.

Value *statements* alone do not establish the value system (the attitude ecosystem) of the company. What matters is what people in the company actually *do*. In other words, implied values are actually more relevant, meaningful, and important than expressed values.

However, it *is* important for a company to have a written statement of values. The process of writing a statement of values is good for communication and shared understanding: it crystallizes ideas and provides an opportunity to discuss what values really mean. The statement of values is sometimes the only opportunity for decision makers in a company to be explicit about their own values *if they mean what they say.*

A written statement of values gives prospective employees an opportunity to assess whether this is a company that they could enjoy working for. It allows the company to be explicit about what is expected. Above all, if everyone takes the stated values seriously as guidelines for everyday behavior, the effort of creating these statements will pay off by bringing the company closer to a unified culture of cooperation and high performance, closer to Culturetopia.

Values Alignment

In Culturetopia, there are no conflicts in the application of values: there is complete and consistent values alignment.

In Culturetopia, there are no conflicts in the application of values. The secret to building an effective attitude ecosystem is easily stated: **create complete and consistent values alignment.** In a company with aligned values, the rider and the elephant want to get to the same place by the same route. Or, to use Jim Collins' metaphor: everyone is on the right bus, and they're sitting in the right seat.

There are several areas in which alignment is essential:

- The stated values of the company must align with principles that are honestly believed by those who state them. Values that are not based on truly held principles are merely words and the values will not stick. In other words: **be honest.**

- The stated values of the company must be aligned with the needs and aims of the company and its workforce. Irrelevant values are either ignored or cause conflicts and confusion. **Be relevant.**

- Stated values should not just be fuzzy notions. The values should be aligned with reality by describing what they mean in practice. **Be explicit.**

- Build a workforce that is in tune with and aligned with the values, by selecting, training, coaching, and reinforcing. Values should not have to be imposed on the workforce; the people in the company should actually be people who are in tune with the values. In building the workforce, **be selective and be persistent.**

- The stated values of the company must be applied equally to customers, suppliers, executives, and other employees. **Be consistent.**

- The actions of the company must be aligned with its stated values. **Walk the talk.**

Culturetopian Values

What are the Culturetopian values with which we need to align? Not all companies are the same, nor do they all operate in the same environment, so their values may be different in their details. However, my experience with multiple companies (some of whom are headed for Culturetopia, others not so much) leads me to believe that there are a few common factors in company values that strongly define their ability to run a high-performance company.

There is no single perfect way to build a house or a nation or a company. That's why there's such a rich and interesting variety out there, and that's a good thing. However, we find that companies that have created a highly productive collaborative working environment share many common features. These are the values that attract talented employees and underpin a company's ability to run a high-performance organization. These are the values that bring the people in the company closer to Culturetopia.

The essential Culturetopian values are:

- In Culturetopia, there is a shared sense of direction and purpose.

- In Culturetopia, customers define the approach to business.

- In Culturetopia, mentors (managers and supervisors) are there to help.

- In Culturetopia, everyone is a leader.

- In Culturetopia, people build sound relationships and high-achieving teams.

- In Culturetopia, everyone has opportunities for learning and growth.

- In Culturetopia, work is satisfying, rewarding, and fun for everyone.

6

A Shared Sense of
Direction and Purpose

In Culturetopia, everyone knows why the company is in business.

Every company must make some very clear pronouncements about itself, the business it's in, and where it is headed. This is normally in the form of a mission statement, although some companies call it a vision statement, and others have both a vision and a mission. It doesn't matter. What is important is that your company makes one or more statements that define:

- **Company purpose**: This is what the company is in business to do, and what it must do to meet the needs, wants, and aspirations of its customers.

- **Company direction**: This is where the company is headed in the near term and more distant future.

- **Company character:** This is an indication of the nature of the company and the people who work for it.

Where does the team mission come from? Generally, the mission originates from the people who were the driving force in the company at the outset — its founders — but the mission should not be immutable. The world changes; new opportunities emerge as older opportunities diminish. The economy changes and the expectations of customers also change. To keep a mission alive, it needs to be reviewed and updated from time to time.

In Culturetopia, everyone understands their individual role and how it contributes to the company's mission.

The mission of the company must cascade in to all levels of the business if it's going to mean anything. Divisions, departments, and teams must have clarity of purpose. The company mission can be divided into bite-sized goals for departments and groups that, together, will drive the whole company towards achievement of the company's mission.

If any group has objectives that are not explicitly linked to the company's mission, they may lead to counterproductive behavior.

Individual employees need a personal mission too: this is more often called a *job description*. If the individual delivers his or her personal mission (in other words, does the job well, as defined) then that contribution will move the whole company closer to achieving the company's mission.

Just like the company mission, individual jobs, team roles, and department missions must be defined in terms of the needs of customers: both internal customers and external customers.

In Culturetopia, everyone acts in ways consistent with the company mission, always.

One big advantage of having clear statements of mission, vision, and values is that it actually makes everyone's job much easier. These statements provide a sound foundation to guide the decisions, actions, and behaviors of every employee at every level.

Once the company has defined its mission, it must be communicated and *actually used*.

Too many companies put the mission statement in a picture frame and forget about it. This is unfortunate, because the mission statement, if it's a good one, can be useful to everyone, every day. But first they need to know what it says! This demands sustained effort from chiefs and mentors who must communicate the mission. They have a duty to explain the mission, justify it, and sell it, so that every employee shares in a common understanding of the mission and of the objectives that the company is aiming to achieve.

However, communication is more than just saying the right words. A common thread in many low-performing companies is that there is a big disconnect between what the company says it's aiming for, and what the employees of those companies actually do at work every day.

Just as every employee's personal values and attitudes should be aligned with company values, their assigned tasks and responsibilities need to be aligned with the mission. Every employee must understand the reasons why their own work is important, and how it contributes to the company mission.

Communicating the mission plus task alignment ensures that everyone acts in ways consistent with the company mission, always.

In Culturetopia, there are standards, and people pay attention to them.

In Culturetopia, there are explicit standards for the

performance of every role in the company, everyone understands those standards and how success is measured, and everyone is trained to meet those standards. In Culturetopia, performance routinely exceeds the targets.

Why are standards important? Because people work better and more productively when they know exactly what is expected of them; when they know what acceptable performance is and what isn't; and when they receive quick and relevant feedback on their performance. Anything that is not made explicit is left to chance. Most employees appreciate clarity, whether it concerns the expected behavior in dealing with a complaining customer, or how much production is expected in a day. Do employees take advantage of lack of clarity? Of course they do, but at least it shows they are thinking. Managers who fail to state expectations clearly should not get angry with their employees for pushing the envelope. On the other hand, some overcautious or overanxious employees might assume that if they aren't told something is permitted, it is forbidden. This stifles creativity and limits productive behavior.

Suppose a well-meaning father tells his small son, "Hey, Justin, don't go too far!" But the little guy has no idea where *too far* is. The dad might want his son to stay in the yard. But if the child is cautious by nature, he'll play within feet of the back door, and miss out on all the exploring in the far corners. A different type of youngster might end up dodging cars in the street. "It wasn't too far for *me*, Dad!"

Setting explicit standards is an essential step in creating an environment in which people can perform well.

The company must make very clear what standards are expected from *every one* of its employees: frontliners, mentors, and chiefs. Where do those standards come from? Standards should not be arbitrary rules imposed by faceless management. Standards must be linked to the mission of each team and department, and that mission, is linked to the needs of internal and external customers. In this way, an understanding of customer needs is an intrinsic part of defining the business.

Standards must prevent behavior that is inconsistent with the company values, yet not limit creative exploration of better ways to do the work.

The company must also define how compliance is measured and must communicate those rules and standards clearly, and often: every day.

A very important element of that communication is to provide employees with the training they need to deliver to those standards: training is one very effective way of being explicit about what is expected. The first day of training for a new recruit is when it all starts; this should be as much a celebration as an information session. New hires should learn right away about the values and standards embraced by everyone in the company, and they should understand that their new job is not just a job — it's an opportunity to contribute to something special. Amazing companies need amazing people, but those people emerge from the ranks of normal employees who respond to the energy and enthusiasm of a Culturetopian company.

Setting standards requires some type of measurement; otherwise, how can you tell if the standards are being consistently achieved? This applies to all mission-critical tasks throughout the company, at all levels. Building a measurement system that is appropriate for the company, that is not overly burdensome and provides useful information for everyone, is something of a science; it's not easy.

However, the measurement system is too important to neglect. In Culturetopia, a good measurement system is a valuable tool for every single company employee, not just for mentors and chiefs. Motivated frontliners use the measurement system to chart their own progress, to pinpoint areas where improvements are needed, and to develop ideas to deliver those improvements.

Once your measurement system is in place, don't just leave it unaltered for years. You want to improve it and then improve it some more.

Keep raising the standard.

If you impressed your customers last year, everyone must work hard to "wow" them even more this year and the next.

7

Customers Define
the Approach to Business

In Culturetopia, everyone understands that customers pay for everything.

At the heart of the most successful companies is the desire, embedded in the company culture, to do great things for their customers. Customers are why companies exist. Customers are the primary source of the income that is used to reward the company's employees (and shareholders).

Everyone knows that happy customers spend more of their money with your company, are loyal, and tell their friends good things about you, which brings even more business.

Without happy customers, companies will die.

So, in Culturetopia, everyone understands that customers pay for everything. Yet, when we look objectively at the behavior of employees at all levels in many of our pre-Culturetopian companies, we see behavior that is not consistent with the idea that taking care of customers is essential. For some people, making customers happy is an optional extra, something they'll do later when they're not so busy.

The first step in delivering outstanding service to customers is to remind everyone, at all levels in the company, where the money comes from. Ultimately, *customers* put food on our tables, clothes in our closets, provide us with shelter, education, surround-sound systems, and so on. This provides a persuasive context for everyone to face the challenge of delivering the best possible service to the customers who keep the company in business.

In Culturetopia, the constant aim of everyone is to establish and maintain a positive and mutually beneficial relationship with customers.

What do we mean when we talk about *world-class* customer service? Sometimes it's difficult to define, but I've experienced it, and I know it when it touches me. I hope you've had some similar experiences.

Have you ever worked with someone who is *totally* a customer service person? Many people try to do customer service jobs, but some people simply perform customer service better, more naturally and more easily than others. This is a skill that is often underrated. Having a talent for customer service is just like having a talent for music or sport: the combination of a natural inclination plus instruction and practice.

From a customer's point of view, what makes world-class customer service? Here is my list; perhaps you can add some more items from your own personal perspective:

- Great customer service primarily delivers the product or the service the customer expects, and a little bit more. Exceeding expectations is a good thing.

- No matter how brief the transaction, the customer should feel that a relationship of warmth exists between himself or herself and the company's representative.

- Everything about the interaction with the customer should reassure the customer that he or she has made the right buying decision.

- The experience should provide good value (whether it costs a lot or a little).

- Things sometimes go wrong. The customer should get the sense that the company is poised to leap into action to help fix any problem (big or small, whatever the cause).

- The customer should feel that he or she is dealing with someone who is empowered to really help.

- When things go wrong, customers expect an apology. A brief apology accompanied by a quick result is much, much better than a long and cringing statement of contrition, with no apparent action to back it up.

If you have never had the good fortune to encounter a customer service experience that was so good you told your friends about it, then you should shop around until you do. If you don't understand the feeling a customer gets from experiencing great customer service, it's not going to be easy for you (or your team) to become great at customer service.

How can we create a business environment in which we deliver world-class customer service, every day?

Constant communication, coaching, and reinforcement of the customer service team is essential.

This concept deserves an entire book, but here are some headlines learned from my many years in the customer service arena:

- Recruit enthusiastic, positive, and friendly service people.

- Hire people who have a natural talent for delivering great customer service.

- Educate every employee in the art of building relationships.

- Treat every customer as if they have just entered *Servicetopia*.

- Train all service people to shock their customers with their hugely friendly, highly competent, and seriously fun approach to service.

- Seize opportunities to impress.

- Train people to listen carefully to gain full understanding of the customer's wants or needs.

- Treat any problem that arises as an opportunity to do great things for the customer.

- Provide customer service employees with the power to seize opportunities to "WOW" the customer.

- Fix problems quickly and completely.

- Provide everyone with the power to solve problems.

- Reward people who find creative solutions.

- Teach employees how to apologize gracefully on behalf of the company, even when it's not their fault.

In Culturetopia, everyone has customers and is a customer.

In Culturetopia, people regard their co-workers as internal customers and as suppliers of internal customer service.

Every individual, team, or department does work for a reason, and that reason is almost always because someone somewhere wants the product of that work. If it isn't directly wanted by a paying (external) customer, then it is almost certainly wanted by someone somewhere else in the company.

In Culturetopia, people take their internal customers seriously. They enter into agreements with each other about what is needed, when it's needed, what level of quality is required, and at what cost. In Culturetopia, jobs are defined by customers.

This is the way that Culturetopia companies answer the question: How can we maintain standards, ensure work quality, and monitor performance without putting in place micro management and bureaucratic systems?

In Culturetopia, we can create a positive and mutually supportive atmosphere of cooperation and accountability throughout the workforce by always linking the work we do to the needs of internal and external customers.

This doesn't mean there's no need for supervision and normal management oversight. But that traditional approach should be seen as more of a safety net in the event of something going seriously wrong than the mechanism to assure good work, day in and day out. In a highly productive workforce *with an unerring commitment to satisfying customers*, quality management, adherence to standards, continuous process improvement, and productivity gains are all built in to the workforce's attitudes towards their jobs and each other.

The chain of supply between individuals, teams, and departments leads ultimately to a paying customer, someone outside the company. The quality and value of products and services provided to the ultimate customer depends entirely on what happens along every link of the chain. The level of service delivered to the external customer can only be as good as the level of service delivered internally, from one team or department to another.

Treating every internal transaction just as seriously as an external customer service transaction, throughout the company and at all levels, motivates people to feel accountable to each other and to hold each other accountable for performance and behavior. People impose their own disciplines on themselves and on each other. This establishes a largely self-monitoring and self-regulating system operated and controlled by the people who do the work, minimizing the need for supervision and external management.

8

Managers are There to Help

In Culturetopia, mentors (managers and supervisors) exist primarily to increase job satisfaction for frontliners.

For some (I hope), this Culturetopian principle will seem to be outrageous. Let me explain the logic.

In traditional, pre-Culturetopian companies, managers generally assumed that people came to work to trade hours for dollars so they could buy food and clothing and shelter. Fear of not getting basic needs met is what made people come to work, and the fear of being fired is what made people do a good job. Employees themselves would usually endorse that view: how many people would stay working in their current job if they won the lottery?

This simplistic view of human motivation was only true in one sense: people made it so, because they said it was so, and behaved in accordance with that assumption.

This, in the nineteenth century and most of the twentieth century, set the pattern for company culture:

managers and company owners assumed that workers did not want to be at work, and so the role of the manager as inspector and police officer quickly emerged. Employees, especially employees of large industrial companies, had little choice but to reflect that view of the world, because (let's face it) many jobs were unattractive, unpleasant, and sometimes dangerous. Many people felt they had little choice but to become a cog in their local industrial machine.

For decades, the tension between management and other employees (the people who actually make things and perform services for customers) has been thoroughly influenced by these nineteenth-century assumptions, even as technology, education, and the aspirations of people have evolved.

Today, it is possible to run organizations with minimal command and control, by allowing well-trained and motivated frontline employees to take responsibility and exercise leadership. And what do managers and supervisors do if they're not commanding and controlling? They become mentors who help and encourage frontliners to take responsibility and exercise leadership.

In Culturetopia, the constant aim of management is to free employees to focus on the task.

What are managers for? One of the most important roles of management is to create an environment that reduces stress and increases task focus for the people who do the real work.

Managers are there to free employees to focus on the task.

In most companies, people don't spend much time actually doing useful work. They consume a lot of time discussing or arguing about what to do, who should do it, and what the result should look like. People also spend a lot of time and energy worrying about where they should sit, what color the walls should be painted, and how much each person should be paid for their work. People argue about who should get the biggest desk, who needs a laptop computer, and who doesn't. People spend time worrying about their children's education, dreaming about their next vacation in Hawaii, writing science fiction novels, or playing FreeCell on their office computer. When things go wrong, they waste time blaming each other instead of fixing the problem and making sure it doesn't happen again.

Also, people worry: Am I doing my job well enough? Does the boss like me? Do my colleagues resent my talents, or do they think I'm clueless? Will I get a promotion? Will I be let go when the end-of-year results are published? Some people are bored in their jobs, have too much time to think, and get stressed thinking about how they are wasting their lives. Others have an apparently endless to-do list and get stressed thinking about how they can find some time to think.

In pre-Culturetopian companies, people spend large chunks of time not doing useful work. There is insufficient focus on the real tasks that need to be done and too much effort dissipated in conflict, argument, and displacement activities. Failing to get the important work done can increase stress even more, because people like to achieve and don't like to fall behind.

> Where people work together to achieve some end
> goal, there needs to be an overriding focus on
> *getting the job done.*

People are complex, thinking organisms, even those who do apparently mundane jobs.

Here's the problem with having thinking, feeling beings doing work in a company: they think and feel and react in subtle and sometimes unpredictable ways. Here's the good thing about having thinking, feeling beings doing work in a company: they think and feel and react in subtle and sometimes unpredictable ways that are sensitive and supportive to the needs of others; this can generate delight and a feeling of warmth in those other thinking, feeling beings who are ultimately the source of income, profits, dividends, and salaries: the customers.

What can a manager do to create a working environment in which employees can focus on the task and on the customer (internal and external customer) and are not distracted by other things? What does a manager do to minimize tension and stress caused by others, so that people can focus on getting the job done?

The main thing a manager can do to help is to guide behavior, by encouraging and rewarding productive behavior and eliminating disruptive behavior. Companies don't have good or bad employees; they have employees whose behavior is good, or whose behavior is bad. Some employees behave consistently in line with company values, others less so. Either way, the reason they are performing the way they are performing is because of the cultural environment that has been created in that company or department. Whether they know it or not, managers generally play a large part in developing that environment, through the way they behave, the guidance they give, the standards they set, the way they reward good behavior, and the way they handle bad behavior.

In Culturetopia, there is no disruptive behavior (and no one misses it).

People feel tension and stress primarily because of the behavior of other people. Some people have personal issues and problems that get in the way of productive behavior. As Robert Sutton elegantly puts it, "A few demeaning creeps can overwhelm the warm feelings generated by hordes of civilized people."

If bad behavior becomes endemic in the culture, then most people will start to behave badly. The culture will win. Somehow, bad behavior tends to spread faster than good behavior. When a muddy dog jumps on a white couch, the couch gets dirty, but the dog doesn't get clean. But positive cultures can win, too. Islands of excellence in a sea of mediocrity *can* actually survive and grow.

In Culturetopia, managers and workers are productive because they are not distracted by conflict, workplace gossip, company politics, or other types of disruptive behavior.

Self-discipline is by far the best form of supervision,

and in Culturetopia (of course), everyone will be productive and behave constructively at all times. But this is the real world, and we are still working towards Culturetopia, so sometimes people behave badly or inappropriately. All employees, not just managers and supervisors, have a responsibility to encourage productive behavior, and that means they also have a responsibility to handle nonproductive behavior as soon as it happens.

Anyone who has worked in or with a pre-Culturetopian company has seen examples, possibly outrageous examples, of workers behaving badly:

- Executives squabbling over boardroom privileges, while no one pays attention to the steady decline in customer satisfaction metrics…

- A manager yelling at some unfortunate employee in front of embarrassed customers…

- Customer service reps chatting about some TV show while a customer waits, losing hope, for some attention…

- Project team members sabotaging an important change initiative…just because they can.

I have dozens more examples. They could fill a book.

Some people might argue that disruptive behavior is merely a symptom of something else wrong in the way the company is being run. Maybe, some people suggest, disruptive behavior is the only way an employee can bring attention to a grievance or to a work problem. This might be the case in some pre-Culturetopian companies, but in Culturetopia, there are better ways of communicating, as we shall see later. In Culturetopia, disruptive behavior serves no useful purpose: it's just, well, disruptive.

Prompt action to address disruptive behavior and its underlying cause is an essential to reduce distress and tension all across the workplace.

In Culturetopia, disruptive behavior is outlawed, and no one misses it. If disruptive behavior appears, managers and co-workers deal with it quickly and effectively.

The essentially cooperative and collaborative environment that is needed to enable people to do their best work does not mean that it's acceptable for managers, supervisors, and executives to be weak and inactive when disruptive behavior occurs. The opposite is the case. An understanding of the dynamics of corporate culture should make it more obvious to managers that disruptive behavior is not just a nuisance, it gets in the way of other people having satisfying and productive working lives. People don't like it when that happens, and sometimes management authority needs to be exercised for the good of everyone else.

Behaviors are either consistent or inconsistent with the standards you have set. When you, as a manager, come across behavior that is not aligned with the company standards, you have to do something about it. Mostly, when employees perform badly, they perform badly because of the environment they're working in. Their environment doesn't encourage or teach them what types of behaviors are appropriate, and what other types of behavior are unproductive or even counterproductive.

My six-year-old daughter has always been full of energy and quite adventurous. When she was three years old, she sometimes climbed on to our glass-topped breakfast table to reach the fruit bowl. She's tall like me, and I was worried she'd fall through. So I'd say, "Laura Lee, you're a good girl, and good girls don't climb on the furniture. You might hurt yourself. So, please get down. Just ask if you want an apple. Thank you." And she'd climb down. I try hard to stay calm, to explain why there's a problem and what to do about it. She *is* good, and I need to understand (and help her understand) that sometimes her behavior is inconsistent with who she really is. (I don't want to do it like my dad. He was a little more immediate with his feedback: "Hey, jackass! Get off the table. Now.")

It's up to me, as a parent, to create an environment in which my children can learn to behave consistent with the values our family believes in and the standards we have set.

Discipline without learning is not useful for developing responsible behavior. After all, the root word in discipline is disciple, which means to teach.

It's the same thing when dealing with frontline employees. You have to give frontliners the opportunity to get aligned with the company values. You can't expect employees all to know this automatically, so coaching, training, and continual supportive communication are all essential if you're going to align frontliner behavior and performance with company standards and objectives. Part of the process is to get employees to understand the alignment between company values and their *own* values and needs. In this way, behaving well and productively is not an imposition: it fits right in with what most people actually want in their working lives. Most people actually *want* to be helpful and productive. At the end of a working day, they want to be satisfied that they've done something useful and significant.

This understanding, that most people want to do a good job, underpins my belief that we should not think of good or bad employees, but focus on good or bad employee behavior. This approach gives us the very best chance of modifying behavior to be productive instead of unproductive, customer-oriented instead of customer-hostile.

* * *

Now, if people are temperamentally unable to fit in with a company culture, then this does not make them *bad*, but it does mean that, by the company's standards, their behavior will be bad. That's bad enough. If people are unable to change, given appropriate encouragement, training, and space to think, then the manager needs to act to remove him or her. Sometimes an employee just won't fit in. Alignment of values and attitudes just isn't going to happen. So, if someone isn't comfortable with a company's culture, they should go to another company. Sometimes, it may be your job as a mentor (manager or supervisor) to *encourage* someone to do just that. Some-times you have to *insist*.

Making tough decisions doesn't necessarily make a person popular with everyone, but that's all right if it builds the right culture.

Tzu-kung said, "Would it be right if a man were liked by all his neighbors?" "No," said the Master. "And would it be right if a man were hated by all his neigh-bors?" "No," said the Master, "It would be better if the good men of the neighborhood liked him, and the bad men of the neighborhood hated him."

In Culturetopia, frontline employees have the tools, materials, and space to do the job well.

An old proverb says, "A bad workman blames his tools." This is often true. But inadequate tools can still prevent a good employee from doing his or her best work. In Culturetopia, frontliners are provided with the tools, materials, and space to do their jobs well. This removes barriers to excellent job performance. At the same time, it means that no one can use poor tools (or inadequate materials, or lack of working space) as an excuse for poor performance.

In Culturetopia, mentors (managers and supervisors) assist this process by becoming well-informed about what is really needed to do every job well. This is not a question of buying just whatever is asked for. It requires research, analysis, and creative thinking. Sometimes, a simple inexpensive tool works better than a more complex, expensive tool. Sometimes, sophistication is needed to maximize performance. Decision makers can only tell the difference by becoming experts, by becoming involved enough in the day-to-day work to really understand the tools, the software, and the facilities that make the difference between adequate performance and great performance.

In Culturetopia, Mentors always set a good example.

In Culturetopia, mentors consistently behave in accordance with the company values and bring a positive attitude to the work environment.

Some managers believe that frontline employees don't pay any attention to them. In reality, the opposite is true. Employees *do* notice when managers behave badly, and will always interpret this as an indication that it's OK for them to behave badly, too. Most people take some notice of criticism and reprimands, but don't necessarily work any better as a result. On the other hand, people respond well when managers help them do their work better. Frontliners feel *lifted* when they work with positive

people who are supportive, enthusiastic, encouraging, and
energizing. Mentors have a responsibility to help with this
lifting.

Most of us spend half our waking lives at work and
don't want to work alongside people who are bad-tem-
pered, vindictive, and selfish. What type of person are
you at work? Do you bring a positive spirit and good
vibrations, or just bitterness and negativity? If you were
one of your employees or co-workers, would you like to
work with you?

Negativity is unhealthy. People can and do become
ill through worry, stress, and lack of self-esteem. Companies are like people in this respect: the more positive the
company's attitude, the better it performs. Negative
managers in a company can make the whole working
environment depressed and unproductive.

___

**Management energy is better spent encouraging good
behavior than penalizing bad behavior.**

___

Your role as a mentor is to lift, inspire, and encourage your frontline employees, not to oppress them.

Mentors should always adhere to the standards and
values espoused by the company. If you don't take those

standards and value statements seriously, why should your employees?

The relationship between people always tends to be symmetrical: people respond best to people who respond well to them. People are more considerate to considerate people. People work harder when they're surrounded by hard-working people.

Being a positive role model is much, much more than avoiding being caught in bad behavior and negativity. Good mentors bring a positive spirit to everything they do. They engender enthusiasm. They develop genuinely caring relationships with the people around them.

At the end of each working day, every employee (and that includes managers) should be able to take pride in his or her behavior during the day. They should know that they've made a difference for the better, for the company, and for everyone around them.

In Culturetopia, Mentors are expected to recruit people who are more talented than themselves.

In traditional companies, it's easy to spot an insecure manager or supervisor. One of the symptoms of insecurity in a manager is one who recruits people who are less talented than he or she is. This is not surprising in a culture that is dominated by blame rather than responsibility, and driven by internal competition more than by collaboration.

Bosses who knowingly surround themselves with people who are experts in their field are building a nucleus of success in the company. Their talented people will become valuable team members, spread knowledge, and, in turn, recruit other talented people. Bosses who recruit less capable people are, likewise, establishing a core of mediocrity, which will also spread.

If, at the very top of the company, the CEO is dominating, controlling, and anxious not to be outshone, then, in due course, the company will be a mediocre company, or a failing company. If the CEO is smart enough to identify people who will bring the right talents to the job and allow them to excel and to take the credit, then the company will be on the right trajectory for continued performance improvement and success.

There is at least one investment company in the U.S. that bases its investments uniquely on following the trajectory of those senior people who aim high when recruiting their teams. These people have a record of building teams of people around them that are capable of doing great things. When one of these builders join a company, it prospers. There are hard-headed investors out there who have found it immensely worthwhile to invest in a company when one of these people joins, and short the stock when he or she leaves.

9

Everyone is a Leader

In Culturetopia, everyone contributes through influencing and innovation.

In Culturetopia, everyone in the company is permitted and encouraged to make a positive leadership contribution by influencing others, innovating, and initiating change.

What is a leader? In traditional companies, leadership is often equated with formal authority. In a traditional company, managers are supposed to be the leaders, and the higher the management position, the more leadership is expected. In Culturetopia, we understand that leadership is linked not to formal authority, but to the ability to make things happen.

The true leaders in any organization are those who actually influence, innovate, and initiate change.

In a creative, productive, performance-culture company we can find leadership happening everywhere, at all levels and in all positions: the customer service rep who has a bright idea that eradicates a recurrent source of customer irritation; the supervisor who creates energy in his team by rewarding great work with homemade cookies; the technologist who comes up with the new product design that makes the company a hot property. Successful companies encourage everyone to exercise leadership.

Managers and supervisors can either encourage leadership everywhere or stifle it. In Culturetopia, chiefs and mentors seize all opportunities to encourage and reward productive behavior, innovation, and creativity (*leadership*) throughout the company.

Leadership is about having ideas and influencing others.

In a performance-culture company, we do not want anyone in the company to be excluded from having ideas and implementing improvements. In Culturetopia, all employees have the potential to contribute in many more ways than simply doing what they're told to do. Everyone's opinion is taken into account, because great ideas can come from anywhere.

It is not the exclusive right of people in senior positions in the company to be leaders. While many board members and executives are creative and influential,

others just do a job. Some shop-floor and customer-
contact employees just do their jobs; others have ideas
and take actions that change the company.

Leader is not a word that should be used in a job title
unless you are prepared to let everyone in the company
use it.

The idea that *leadership* permeates the organization
and that everyone can and should exercise leadership is
somewhat alien to managers who adhere to traditional
models of running a complex organization. Those managers have been raised to have low expectations of their
employees, and funnily enough, their employees usually
meet those low expectations. Outside the narrow sphere
of running a business, we are becoming more and more
aware of the performance-limiting effect of low expectations and the performance-enhancing effect of combin-
ing high expectations with the tools to do the job.

Children learn new facts and skills when educators
provide an environment in which they are helped to learn,
rather than one in which they sit passively and are only
taught. In raising a family, we find that encouragement,
positive reinforcement, advice, and support provided with
love work a whole lot better than yelling and criticizing.
We all must know someone who passively serves time in

his or her day job, only to become alive, enthusiastic, and highly productive in some voluntary effort. Aid agencies around the world know that the best way to restore relative prosperity to an impoverished village is not just to hand over food and clothing, but to give people the tools to help themselves.

In the education of children, raising a family, engaging people's enthusiasm for helping others, or aiding the Third World, we have learned that providing ordinary people with the space, opportunity, and tools to help themselves can produce extraordinary results.

Many managers spend much time and energy in a quest for the secret to motivating workers to do better. Here it is:

Success is what generates the motivation to be more successful.

Start the process by encouraging employees to work together to produce their best work, give them the tools and training to succeed, and encourage everyone to be a leader. Some level of success follows quite naturally. Recognizing and rewarding that success gives people a buzz that is highly motivating and leads to even better performance. Thus starts the upward spiral of continuous improvement.

In Culturetopia, leaders hold themselves accountable and seize responsibility.

In Culturetopia, leaders (that is, all influencers) take responsibility and promote accountability. They challenge the victim mentality and encourage everyone to take ownership of problems.

Most companies have an organization chart with a CEO at the top who has a lot of power within the company and that power lessens as you move down to the frontline workers. There's nothing wrong with structuring a company like this, but you can't allow employees at any level to begin to think they have no power. When employees feel powerless, they begin to use their influence in negative ways that result in frustration, anger, and eventually apathy. Left unaddressed, a victim mentality begins to form and dominate the culture. If victim thinking is tolerated, it insidiously reinforces an unproductive culture.

Sometimes victims really are victims, sometimes they are just people who feel victimized; it doesn't really matter. The feeling of victimization comes from being blamed. So what's wrong with being blamed, you might ask? If you do something wrong, surely someone has to tell you, make sure you feel the blame? What could be more natural? Blaming is when someone assigns responsibility to someone else. Blaming places the responsibility over there and not over here. The idea is that it's better for someone else to be responsible, because when things go wrong, then *I* can't be blamed. This is all quite normal in a traditional management culture. Surely we can't live without blame, and victims to point at.

In Culturetopia, the expectations are all reversed. Leaders accept responsibility. Leaders realize that when they blame others, they actually lose personal power and weaken the entire organization. So when they point fingers, they point to themselves and acknowledge errors, freely and openly. Others don't need to accuse or to hide. Instead, they can focus on how they can help others to not make the same mistake.

In a culture where people assertively accept responsibility, people learn faster and everyone performs better.

That's right: when everyone holds themselves accountable and seizes responsibility, this creates an atmosphere that drives continuous performance improvement.

A simple example will help to make this clearer. Let's say my boss, Jen, asked me to take the daily deposit to the bank. She reminded me that it needed to be at the bank by 2:00 p.m. to be credited to our account the next day. I said I would be happy to make the trip; I'd done it many times before and I knew about the deadline. Then, on the way to the door, I got a call: a customer problem, really urgent. I saw Jim heading to the door just ahead of me... "Hey, Jim, can you run by the bank for me?" "Sure, it's on my way home."

Next morning, I walked in and saw Jen on the phone ... it was the bank. Then I heard, "Jason! Get in here. What on earth happened to the deposit? The money won't hit our account until tomorrow now."

You can imagine what would happen next in most companies:

Jason: Not my fault, I asked Jim to make the deposit.

Jim: I got it there as soon as I could. I had to pick up my daughter from school because she was sick and then I went to the bank. I got there long before closing. It's Jason's fault; he never told me it had to be in by 2:00 p.m.

Jason: Yes, I did ... I ... I'm sure I told you!

Jim: I'm sure you didn't!

Jen: You're both to blame and I'm writing this up and putting you both on notice!

Jim: Why don't you use the electronic deposit feature at the bank anyway?!

At the end of the discussion, blame has ruined their collective relationship, trust is destroyed, and everyone feels bad. No one is focused on the problem with the bank and no one has done anything to make sure the problem doesn't happen again. Jim won't offer to go to the bank again: he'll always be busy with something else. Jason won't give priority to a customer problem because he'd rather keep Jen happy than spend time doing something she doesn't know is happening. Jen won't ask any favors any more, because she no longer feels she has a sound relationship with her co-workers.

How would this scene play out in a Culturetopian company?

Jen: Jason, what on earth happened to the deposit? The money won't hit our account until tomorrow now.

Jason: Oh, that's not good. My apologies, Jen, I don't know how that could have happened. Let me make a call and then I'll come see you.

Jason: Hi, Jim. Did you make it to the bank with the deposit yesterday?

Jim: I sure did. I had to pick my daughter up from school and then I went straight to the bank. I deposited the check around 3:45 p.m., long before the bank closed. I have the slip.

Jason: I forgot to tell you it had to be there by 2:00 p.m. My error. Don't worry about it, I'll tell Jen what happened.

Jim: Look, I should have told you I planned to go by the school first. Besides, I've dropped off the deposit before...It's part my fault too. I'll come with you to Jen's office.

Jason: Jen, I had a customer issue, so asked Jim to do it but I didn't tell him about the deadline.

Jim: Yeah, but I should have known it had to be there by 2:00 p.m.

Jen: Thanks for explaining what happened. It looks as if both of you assumed too much, but then this would never have been a problem if I'd set up the new electronic bank account so our clients can wire the money directly to the bank. Actually, I'm not sure yet what to do to make that happen. I've never done it before.

Jim: Ah. I can help out there. I used to fix all that stuff in my old job. Let me show you what to do.

At the end of the discussion, everyone is still on good terms, their relationship actually became stronger, and they will willingly work together in the future. Everyone has increased their own power, become just a little bit wiser, and a small process improvement is about to occur.

In Culturetopia, every error becomes a learning experience, because leaders accept responsibility. Repeat this hundreds of times in a company and you build an environment where people become continuously smarter and where the method of working improves every day. Is that good for business, or what?

A culture of blame diminishes the power of everyone, leading to a business that fails to prosper. Accepting responsibility means acquiring leadership power, because it creates the ability to change things for the better.

Leadership power increases when you take responsibility and refuse to blame.

10
Sound Relationships and High-Achieving Teams

In Culturetopia, relationships form the foundation for business success.

What happens when people have friends at work and employees feel that other people in the workplace care about them? Productivity happens.

Sometimes people tell you that you can't be a friend and work effectively together, it's too much of a conflict, and you won't be able to objectively contribute to your team. People who hold that opinion are usually rooted in the type of corporate culture that emphasizes blame rather than accountability, and focuses on personalities instead of productivity. That type of culture has high people-tension, and personality conflicts tend to dominate over task orientation. In that type of unproductive (pre-Culturetopian) culture, it's probably true that developing friendships is not practical or sensible. People who advise you to avoid friendships in the workplace might be right, in *their* workplace.

But if you and the leaders in your company are building and strengthening a performance culture instead of a conflict culture, then the rules of behavior change, and change for the better.

In a performance culture, you *should* try to develop friendships with employees, and encourage people to make friendships with others. What's the benefit of friendship in the workplace? Here are three good reasons:

- People would rather let down a boss than let down a friend.

- Friendship lowers *people-tension* and moves the focus towards the task and away from coping with problematic interpersonal relationships.

- People have more fun and work together more effectively if they are friends.

It's important that the friendship grows from a foundation of mutual respect, trust, and a common desire to do good work in the workplace. Real friendships can grow in the right working environment: in a performance culture, which is conducive to cooperation, focusing on the task, and doing good work. But friendships alone cannot *create* such an environment. In fact, if friends work together in a place where hostility is an everyday part of the company culture, then either their friendship can be damaged or their friendship can get in the way of performance.

Even in a performance culture, you need to be aware of some ways in which friendships can increase people-tension, and pollute your culture by introducing conflicts. Be aware of this risk. If you behave according to the following principles, you and your friends will all benefit from the relationships and so will your company:

- Don't recommend people for hire just because they are your friends. Recommend people who have the right skills, attitude, and temperament to deliver the mission.

- Do not play favorites. Work consistently to deliver the mission in accordance with the values.

- When people get things wrong, focus on the task and the way it is executed, not on the person.

- Friendships emerge from relationships. Be confident that the right friendships will grow naturally, and never rush or force things.

Once again, this reminds us that it is the primary job

of mentors to create the right environment: the performance culture. One of the results of creating a good working culture is the potential for the emergence of real friendships in the workplace, which, in turn, lead to better work from everybody.

Here's another thing to bear in mind. There's now evidence that people who build and sustain lasting relationships actually live longer.

In Culturetopia, sound relationships result in effective teams which are recognized and nurtured as a source of motivation, productivity, creativity, and valuable innovation.

What is a *team*? *Teamwork* and *team spirit* appear in all sorts of different groups of people working together. Companies decide to formally label some of these groups as teams. Other groups may not be given the formal title, but they are teams just the same. There are more varieties of team than you might think and all are important in the creation of a healthy company culture.

Some teams are groups of people who work together every day over the long term, with everyone performing much the same task, sometimes independently, often with the support of others. In this category, we have groups like the service agents for an airline, the customer service reps in a phone company's call center, and the retail assistants in an electronics store. The people in these teams are specialists, but within each team, they're mostly the same type of specialist. These teams range in size from two to maybe hundreds of people. Being a part of this team is the context in which these people do their everyday work, so I describe them as *workplace teams.*

Some workplace teams are different. They are groups of people who work together every day, over the long term, with each individual playing a *specific and well-understood role.* Examples include a construction crew, a fire/rescue crew, a company board, a company chief, and his or her immediate support people. Being on a team is the way they do their everyday work; their work is specialized, and each person in the team is a different type of specialist, so I describe them as *specialist workplace teams.*

Workplace teams operate over an indefinite term: the engagement and commitment is open-ended. This is simply part of business as usual, and the idea is to deliver the results the business needs, every day.

Workplace teams are not the only game in town. There are also *project teams.*

Project teams come together to achieve a focused objective, and once that is achieved, the team no longer exists (or is given a new assignment). A company can create *formal* project teams, with well-defined scope, objectives, and team membership, to deliver a tangible result for the company, for example: the implementation of a new office computer system; the development of an improved process flow; or the launch of an important new line of products. Formal teams have a project mentor and are visibly accountable for what they do. (Giving a project team a code name is one way for chiefs to tell everyone a formal project is important.)

Project teams can also be *informal, such as* when a group of people in the workplace get together to fix a problem, invent something new, or just build relationships so that everyday work flows more smoothly. Informal project teams can deliver enormous benefits for a company, but a company cannot make them happen. A company can only create an environment in which people want to work together to make things better, and then the informal project teams will start to form. Improvements will happen without anyone at the top of the company asking for them.

A proliferation of productive informal projects is a hallmark of a healthy company culture. In Culturetopia, there are lots of informal projects, even though people don't call them by that name. What we see is simply a number of different groups of people working together, improving the way the company does business, and enjoying themselves in the process.

All four types of team have their place. Workplace teams, specialist workplace teams, formal project teams, and informal project teams all deliver valuable benefits in different ways. In Culturetopia, all of these teams exist and interplay. In Culturetopia, all types of teams are engaged, recognized, and *rewarded*.

* * *

You can see I use the word *team* more freely than some people. In fact, the way I see it, if you work in a modern complex business, it's really difficult not to be a member of at least one team. This is why understanding team dynamics and behavior is not an optional extra; it's an essential qualification for anyone interested in running a successful business today.

Why are teams so important to the success of a business? One reason is because of the power of *synergy*. Synergy is when the whole is more than the sum of the parts. We know from practical experience, over and over, that the combined efforts of the members of a team add up to more than the sum of the contributions of the individual team members. Team synergy is what makes 1 + 1 = 3, or even 5. Why be content with 2 when you can get 5 from the same people?

The concept of synergy is not unique to teamwork. Examples of synergies are all around us in nature and human endeavor:

- A given amount of proteins, chemicals, and water in a random heap is not the same thing as when the equivalent materials are organized into a creature such as a horse or a bird or a human being.

- A pile of bricks and concrete becomes much more useful when they are organized into the shape and form of a house.

- A business achieves more through the organized collaboration of people than those same people could achieve all working independently with no coordination.

In all these examples, component parts work together to produce something more than the sum of the parts. And the key word in each of these examples is the word *organized*.

The power of synergy means that a team of individuals can deliver results faster and better than the same
individuals could if they were working in isolation.
However, this requires that the team should be more than
a group of individuals: it should be *organized as a real team.*
To become a team, the people have to be aligned with a
common objective, shared information, a defined way of
working together, and *team spirit.*

When team spirit is really working, team members
reach collective decisions that help the team achieve its
mission. Expressing individual points of view is an
essential part of the process, but once the team makes a
joint decision, everyone buys in. Team members realize
that teamwork is about making a contribution, but not
necessarily about getting everything you want.

Team synergies create energy and enthusiasm, too.
One of the most fun times in my working life was when I
was a member of a project team where we worked almost
non-stop for six weeks to deliver a new training program
for frontline supervisors. We organized ourselves based
on strengths and everyone worked hard, twelve hours a
day, six days a week, and we were happy to do it. Team
dynamics provided incentive and support through a really
challenging project. Our achievements were noticed and
rewarded! Everyone in the team would have done the

same thing again if we were faced with the same challenge.

Some companies base their entire way of doing business on the power of teams. Google, for example, gives their developers a lot of freedom to choose the teams they will join, and the teams themselves can decide who to recruit. The result of this apparently haphazard approach is that the power of synergy is given full play. In practice, not just in theory, companies like Google benefit from the high-performing engine of team synergy, which delivers measurably higher levels of creativity, productivity, and job satisfaction.

Team spirit, team commitment, and team success all lead, quite naturally, to create a company culture of collaboration, commitment, personal accountability, and responsibility. In other words: *closer to Culturetopia.*

11
Opportunities for Learning and Growth

In Culturetopia, mistakes and failures are used as opportunities for everyone to learn how to do things better.

There is a big difference between an employee who behaves badly or unproductively, and an employee who tries hard, with the best of intentions, and fails. People make mistakes because they are inexperienced, or are inadequately trained or simply not suited to the work they are doing.

We live in a culture that too often equates failure, in any form, with being a loser. Okay, it's possible to never fail at anything if you never try anything. Coming in second is often dismissed as being as bad as coming in last. Often, the people who do the dismissing are just sitting on a couch watching TV. Is it better to come in second, or to be so far away from success that you just sit and watch someone else trying to achieve something?

In Culturetopia, we regard the occasional failure as an essential part of the learning and development process.

We create controlled opportunities for people to stretch their capabilities, recognizing the possibility of failure. Culturetopia can be a scary environment sometimes. We remove barriers and so allow people to do new things and experiment. When a barrier is taken away, people can sometimes drive off the road, so we make sure the road is not alongside a cliff.

We recognize the inevitability of errors and mistakes and make sure that we separate failure from blame. This makes it easier to avoid the loss of confidence that too often accompanies failure, and allows us to restore people to useful, productive work immediately; it's all part of business as usual in Culturetopia.

In Culturetopia, people are able to focus on doing the type of work they do best.

A Culturetopian company always makes the best use of people's strengths and finds ways to work around their weaknesses.

If you want to be good at something, then practice. One researcher discovered that, to become *world-class* at just about anything, an individual should work at it for four hours a day, six days a week, for ten years. We can clearly see how this applies to musicians, athletes, and other star performers. But it seems to apply equally to stockbrokers, lawyers, plumbers, electricians, writers, and customer service representatives.

Understanding this puts the concepts of *natural talent* and *practice* in some perspective. No matter how much natural talent people have, it's not going to come to anything if they don't practice. On the other hand, individuals with very little natural talent can, in fact, acquire a good level of skill if they just stick to it. But why should people invest all that time and effort in something they don't enjoy doing?

Managers can and do try to encourage or coerce employees into doing things they don't particularly enjoy doing, and sometimes we all have to do things we'd prefer not to do. But surely, whenever we can, it's better, more efficient, and more effective to find out what each person enjoys doing and encourage him or her to do more of it?

There is a component of natural talent that is as much about the joy and satisfaction derived from the activity as sheer physical ability. For a natural musician, playing music is fun in itself. Doing it more increases skill and that creates even more fun.

Job satisfaction is a concept we all understand and is linked to these two astoundingly simple principles:

- People are more likely to engage in an activity if they enjoy it.

- People are likely to enjoy an activity more as they become better at doing it.

This is self-evidently true for *recreational* activities. (I've found no one who will argue that point with me.) Think of tennis or poker or trout fishing or Sudoku. It's a small leap to realize that it's equally true for many creative and sporting jobs: golf pro, musician, chef, sculptor, and baseball pro.

It's only another small leap to recognize that the exact same principles apply to just about every other job ever invented: customer service rep, restaurant server, assembly line worker, help desk technician, sales person, plumber, attorney, and so on.

For business managers, the message should be clear. If you want people to be good at what they do, you have to provide them with the opportunity to develop their talents by working hard at it over a period of time, supported by the right tools, training, and coaching. For people to continue to apply themselves to the task during this learning curve, they must actually enjoy what they are doing. Otherwise, the learning curve will take forever.

* * *

People who enjoy doing something are not only good at it, whatever it is, but have the greatest potential to be even better at it. Don Clifton, in his book *Sour With Your Strengths,* provides a dramatic example of this. Two groups of people were provided with speed reading training. The first group had modest reading ability, averaging 90 words per minute. The second group consisted of quite fluent readers, with an average speed of around 300 words per minute. Clearly the first (low-performing) group had the most room for improvement. After attending the same six-week speed reading course, the low-performing group had improved from 90 to 130 words per minute, a significant and encouraging increase (44 percent). However, the second group, already performing at 300 words per minute before the training, increased their rate to 1,500 words per minute: a 400 percent improvement.

We have all seen similar examples in our own workplaces. I can tell when someone is fully engaged with the task and approaches the challenge with enthusiasm and alertness. People like that quickly absorb new information about the job and grow faster than the people around them. We have also seen people who are dull at work but come alive in some other context: volunteer work, some social environment, or a challenging leisure activity.

> When people act in ways that use their strengths and talents, they grow exponentially.

Most people have something about which they can become enthusiastic or even passionate. Too bad that so many people find so little to enthuse them in their places of work.

Unfortunately, in most traditional workplaces, the individual employee has very little scope or power to change the nature of the work to play to his or her strengths. But managers *do* have that power. By consciously building a working environment and a company culture that recognizes the need for individuals to be enabled to do satisfying work matched to their talents, company owners and mentors can dramatically improve the performance of individuals and the productivity of the company.

* * *

In recent years, there have been significant steps in understanding what makes human beings happy and satisfied.

Traditional psychology tended to focus on what was *wrong* with people and trying to find ways to make them less defective. This newer focus, on *positive psychology*, attempts to understand what makes people perform well as human beings and suggests ways in which their potential can be developed for their own good, and indeed to the benefit of everyone around them, including their work co-workers.

Empirical evidence seems to show that, from each individual's perspective, the following statements are true:

- While the nature of a person's work is not the only determinant of happiness, it is very important.

- Different people are happy in different jobs.

It follows that one important step in achieving a *good life* (Seligman) is to understand your own talents, and put yourself in a position to draw on them. Satisfaction and high performance flow from knowing your strengths, developing them, and using them. If you're going to spend a large chunk of your life doing any single thing, it must be something that you enjoy and are good at.

For example, I am a trainer. Years ago, I learned that training is something I enjoy and I'm good at it. I've tried other roles and I've performed well in most of them, but I keep coming back to training. Give me an accounting job or a regular line supervision job and I'll quickly become frustrated and lose energy. To restore my enthusiasm I'll turn any job, as much as I can, into a training job. It seems that I cannot *not* be a trainer. Today, no matter what I call it (consulting, problem investigation, writing), everything I do becomes a training mission, one way or another.

I even do that at home, and my wife doesn't much like it. She'll say, "Don't you train me!" And I reply, "I can't help it - that's how you *should* load the dishwasher." She knows how to fight back: anything I think I can do better, she gives me as a chore. (That's why I tell people I run things in my house: I run the dishwasher, the vacuum cleaner, and the washing machine.) So that's how she stops me from turning everything into a training opportunity. I suppose people can get too much of a good thing.

* * *

Employees soon find out what they like to do and what they don't. Some people find themselves getting great satisfaction (and earning good money) doing things that many other people couldn't imagine doing every day.

I heard an interview with a clean-up worker whose job is to clear the debris from houses damaged by hurricane Katrina. This is hard work and it can be dangerous, yet this man clearly had pride in his work and enjoyed doing it. While I might get a small sense of satisfaction once in a while when I tidy my desk, this professional clean-up expert transforms chaos and mess into something clean and safe, every working day, and loves it.

We need to give people opportunities to find out what they're good at.

And when someone is not enjoying work (after a reasonable time to get into it), then it's a waste of his or her time and the company's money to insist that the worker struggle on.

In Culturetopia, employees receive the coaching, training, and encouragement they need to do their best work.

In some companies, training is a cost (to be minimized). For some employees, training is a chore to be avoided, unless it happens to be less of a chore than actual work.

In Culturetopia, everyone understands and appreciates the value of knowing how to do things really, really well. Mentors have adequate budgets to spend on carefully planned and targeted training. Because the training is directly relevant to the work, frontliners welcome it. As frontliners exercise their skills, they get continuous constructive feedback from mentors and co-workers.

Then, if an enthusiastic frontline employee enjoys being (for example) a customer service rep, then he or she will obtain double satisfaction and enjoyment from being a well-trained service rep, confidently able to handle just about any challenge. Why should work be any different from any other human activity? It's not. Remember our two principles from the last section?

- People are more likely to engage in an activity if they enjoy it.

- People are likely to enjoy an activity more as they become better at doing it.

Earlier, we focused on the first principle. Now think about the second one. This principle explains why job training and constructive feedback is even more important than we used to think it was. It's not simply about doing the job better: it's part of the virtuous spiral of improved skills leading to more enjoyment, leading to even more skills ... and so on.

12

Work is Satisfying and Rewarding for Everyone

In Culturetopia, people are rewarded for producing results.

Success is its own reward, to a surprisingly large extent. However, if the success is a hidden secret, it will soon cease to be so motivating. Therefore, success and achievement must be rewarded.

The purpose of rewards is not to motivate people to be successful.

The purpose of rewards is to celebrate success and to reinforce and multiply the natural buzz that everyone gets from being successful.

Individual contributions must be recognized and rewarded. However, if we are serious about leveraging the power of teams (as we discussed earlier, in Chapter 10), then we should aim to reward individuals in the context of their contribution to teams, as well as when they do something notable as a soloist. After all, the best results usually come from effective collaboration by talented individuals, not from a single star performer. This is work, not showbiz. (But even rock stars need others: sound engineers, session musicians, roadies, and people who organize events and sell the tickets.)

If you want to encourage team behavior, then reward team success.

If rewards are focused *only* on individual performance, then individuals will *only* be motivated to do what is necessary to shine, even if it gets in the way of team performance.

This is a difficult notion for some managers to get their minds around. Our entire culture is oriented towards the celebration of the individual. Now, this would be fine if the success of the company depended only on the behavior of individuals, aggregated in some way. But this is not how organizations work.

Why do I believe teams are a good thing? It's because the combined efforts of the members of a team add up to more than the sum of the separate contributions of the team members. This is *synergy*, which I discussed earlier.

By focusing *only* on individuals, managers are choosing to forego the synergistic benefits of teams. In a performance culture, in Culturetopia, company chiefs and mentors focus rewards and recognition on team behavior and team results and on individual contributions within the team context, because that's where the synergies are, that's where the big payoffs are. What gets rewarded gets repeated.

Every company should have a well-understood and consistent approach to recognition and rewards: it's an essential component in the Culturetopian set of values.

Rewarding team behavior and rewarding individuals appropriately in a team context is a complicated topic. However, in this section I will set out some basic guidelines concerning the nature of team and individual rewards, and how teams and people should be chosen for rewards. I'll also mention briefly the special needs of large workplace teams, in which team dynamics may be somewhat different.

* * *

First, let's make it clear that when we talk about rewards in Culturetopia, this is not just about financial rewards. Financial rewards can play a part: hardly anyone says no to more money. But tangible, non-financial rewards are often appreciated even more than the financial equivalent, simply because it takes more thought and consideration to choose those rewards.

True, it doesn't take a lot of effort for a sales manager to offer a prize of a vacation in Hawaii to the top salesperson. It's been done before and that kind of thing is just another way of giving a financial reward, maybe with a tax benefit. I'm more interested in how imagination and a clear understanding of what employees really value can come into play in a dynamic and fun way.

I once surveyed employees to find out what type of simple (non-financial) rewards would be appreciated and valued by the members of the team. The number one response was flexibility in their work schedules. Our customer service employees bid for their schedules based on seniority and once the schedule was set, it stayed in place for months. To create flexibility, we allowed for shift trades and position trades with advance approval. We also developed a way of rewarding special contributions to team performance with *free day cards*: these enabled frontliners to be off the work schedule for a free day on short notice. The value of this prize to the service rep was much greater than the actual cost to the company and it became a more enduring method of rewarding individual and team contributions.

Number two on the list was food. We would routinely reward great teamwork with pizza parties or with doughnuts in the morning. To equip our supervisors with tools to lower tension and recognize contributions to the team, we traded with the local frozen yogurt shop for coupons for small cups of frozen yogurt. It worked great. We discovered that rewarding people on the spot had tremendous impact on morale and energy. Whenever we observed someone doing something just right, or spectacularly well, we'd provide an instant reward with a frozen yogurt coupon and an extra break. *Good job! That's exactly how we want to treat our customers! Go and have a frozen yogurt on me.* This is something you should use strategically; you don't want to overuse it or it loses its impact. A smart mentor will stay in tune with the frontliners and look for creative ways to reward employees by doing something different the next month. But the payback on the investment in frozen yogurt for a few weeks was visible and lasting.

Rewards can take many forms: money; food, drinks, candy (not too much candy please); tickets for movies, theater, concerts; gift cards for restaurants; shopping vouchers; and more. The more thought you put into the reward, the more it will be appreciated.

But whatever the tangible reward, please note: rewards in themselves seldom reinforce good behavior in the longer term unless they are linked to performance standards and accompanied by recognition and celebration. Rewards need to make people feel good.

In Culturetopia, everyone seizes opportunities to *celebrate achievement.* Celebrate when the team meets the customer service targets. Celebrate every time someone does something special for a customer. Celebrate productivity improvements. Also, just as you would do in your family, celebrate births, birthdays, and important life events. Someone earns a college diploma by working nights and weekends or runs a marathon for charity? Celebrate those things, too. All celebration reinforces and accelerates the spiral of improvement.

* * *

How do you know who to reward? Which teams and individuals should be rewarded?

You know what kind of company you want to build, so the overriding principle is this: reward those behaviors that lead towards your vision for the company.

Beyond this, here are some more specific guidelines

that I have found useful over many years of working with teams, large and small, in many different companies:

Rewards should be seen to be fair. It's impossible to be fair if you don't have some standards for rewards that are applied consistently. Recurring rewards (those that you award every week or month or year) should always be based on *known objective standards, applied consistently*. If you give a reward for "best baggage handling team of the month," then make sure that the criteria for being chosen are explicit and clear, so that people know exactly what to aim for. And don't drop the award after just a couple of months: if it's important, then it should become part of the way your business runs long-term.

Reward consistent success. Don't restrict rewards just to the *best*. If you set goals for teams and they consistently achieve those goals, then *every* team that exceeds the standard should get a reward of some sort.

Reward loyalty and model behavior. Sometimes people make a contribution in a quiet way, just by being there, doing the job, and not causing strife. It's good to recognize model behavior: perfect attendance records, perfect timekeeping, long (and useful) service to the company.

Don't forget the unsung heroes. We often focus

too much on firefighters: people in the company who fix big problems (which, in some cases, they might have actually caused in the first place). Don't forget the quiet triumphs and achievements of less public teams and individuals, such as the team in the back office who worked all weekend to make up for a broken computer system; the accounts payable team whose efforts fixed the company's cash flow problem; and the procurement and logistics staff that makes sure that every spare part arrives in time to ensure no customer is kept waiting.

Reward brilliance. Sometimes teams or individuals do something really special, something outside the realm of normal expectation. If this special effort helps the company be better in any way, reward it. This could be a new invention, a change to a process that saves time and money, or a way to avoid a long-standing problem that's been annoying to customers.

Use objective metrics. It's also not possible to be fair if you don't know what's going on throughout the company. Objective information is, therefore, an essential input to the process, and when rewards are based on measured performance, you'd better make sure that the measurements are not only accurate, but that they're relevant, too.

Gather opinions, too. In some cases, concrete, objective information may not be enough. You need some opinions, too, but especially for big rewards, one opinion is seldom enough (even if you are the CEO). *Seek multiple opinions.* People throughout the company and at all levels can be asked to comment on which teams made a difference. Some companies actively involve team members themselves in the reward decisions. People in teams know whom among their co-workers made a good contribution and who helped the team achieve results. All of these inputs can be used to both reward each team as a team and to reward individuals for their contribution to teams and to the company.

* * *

When teams are fairly small and well-defined, then understanding the importance of team dynamics and how to reward achievement is quite straightforward. This is the case for most specialist workplace teams and for project teams.

However, when workplace teams are very large (for example, an entire department of several hundred people), it's not easy to apply the same rules. It's a fact of human nature that, while people can identify with large groups (even with whole companies), daily behavior is more closely linked to the dynamic relationships between an individual and the relatively small number of people they interact with every day.

To build team spirit within a large group and obtain the benefits of team synergy, mentors responsible for the operations of such large workplace groups must make special efforts to *create small-team interactions* within the larger team.

For example, when some important change to the workplace is needed, create a *formal project team* of individuals from across the workplace. It's sometimes possible for such teams to be largely self-selecting and self-managing, and when a formal project team receives a reward from the company, the team can work out how to spread the reward around.

Here's another suggestion: a collaborative set of relationships can also be nurtured by engendering team spirit among an almost arbitrary group, for example, by celebrating with one event all the people who have just achieved an academic success or sporting success or had children in the past month.

Sometimes you can encourage team spirit in a large workplace team by having fun with performance awards. One time, I offered a team prize to the best-performing team of ten people, but I didn't tell anyone who was on which team. Then, the following month, I moved people around to different teams. Such *ghost teams* can, in fact, be effective in ramping up overall levels of large group performance. This is because it adds the possibility of a significant reward to the equation. I've tried it and it works.

* * *

In Culturetopia, employees enjoy the working environment.

In Culturetopia, people work in pleasant and stimulating surroundings. The buildings, furniture, décor, and tools create a comfortable, pleasant, and productive physical working environment.

I can hear some (pre-Culturetopian) readers thinking: *People shouldn't go to work to have fun, they go to work to work. Why spend money on a pleasant working environment?* Well, I could point to loads of research that shows convincingly the positive effect that the physical environment has on mood and attitude. Mood and attitude have a direct impact on individual and team performance.

Clearly, C-level people in companies believe they need to have pleasant offices with views and artwork in order to create a working environment that is conducive to good work. Otherwise, why would they spend money on such things? However, why do many of those same decision makers believe that the nature of the environment does not figure in the productivity of other employees in the company? Thankfully, the need to provide reasonable conditions for all frontline workers is becoming increasing recognized. This is not simply because it's fair and civilized (which it is) but also because good working conditions measurably increase productivity.

More and more, in successful and ambitious companies, we see serious attention being applied to artifacts: uniforms, furniture, artwork, décor, and building design from the perspective of increasing pleasure and productivity, both at the same time.

Back in the early 1990s, Southwest Airlines Co. was experiencing growing pains. Staff numbers had doubled, thanks to the fantastic success of the company in penetrating new markets and winning and retaining customers with its innovative approach to customer service. Part of the secret (not such a big secret) of that success was the *culture of friendliness and helpfulness* that embraced all customers who flew with Southwest. However, as the company grew bigger, it required a conscious effort to maintain that attitude of fun and friendliness.

One important element in achieving this was a
deliberate and sustained effort to ensure that every
employee understood the company's history and culture,
and had a voice in creating and maintaining that culture in
the future. Employees were actively involved in this effort
by getting to participate in *Culture Committees* that made
real decisions about the working environment. This
included fresh new décor, attractive and comfortable
uniforms (that the people actually liked to wear), and
homey touches, such as pictures of families on the walls.
None of these decisions cost much money, but the effort
to make sure the environment matched the mood the
company wanted to create paid off, and continues to do
so.

Many other companies are achieving tangible gains
by paying attention to the physical environment. The
RadioShack corporation's headquarters in Fort Worth is
light, spacious, and boldly decorated. Employees I talked
to there love the space and tell me it promotes collaboration and energizes the whole working atmosphere.
Starbucks pays close attention to making the working
environment comfortable and friendly, even in the small-
est coffee shop. Comfortable and friendly surroundings
make it easier for employees to be friendly to the custom-

ers. Google obtains great productivity and creativity from its analysts and programmers by providing great facilities (and excellent free food). They are an important part of the Google formula.

Mentors and chiefs are the people who must support the frontliners by creating a working environment that supports high productivity, not one that gets in the way.

In Culturetopia, everyone feels that their everyday work is worthwhile: it's not a waste of their time or their lives.

Ask the boss or the owner of a company what a *good* company culture is, and he or she will probably say it's a productive one: a place where people can work well and generate profitable revenues.

Why do people come to work? A *New York Times* survey found that *recognition* came out on top of the list. Second was the nature of the work itself. Both these factors were seen as more important than compensation (which came in at fourth most important on the survey) and benefits (third). Employees want to feel that their work is worthwhile and recognized as such. Why should someone spend more than forty hours a week doing something that they feel is not significant or relevant? To get a pay check? That's about it.

It seems that just about everyone would rather do useful work than waste his or her time. People generally prefer to make other people happy, or even delighted, rather than annoy and frustrate them.

People want to be satisfied at the end of a day's work, not just tired and frustrated.

I have stated elsewhere that alignment of what the company wants and what employees want is essential if you want to run a successful company. The closer the alignment, the more the company will prosper. The great news is that most employees are aligned with the company on this topic.

Employers want employees to do useful work. Employees want to do useful work. So where is the problem? The problem lies in managers who ignore the reality that employees want to be useful. By assuming that employees have no interest in doing good work, and no desire to experience the buzz of achievement, managers miss out on big opportunities to allow their employees to do their best work.

In Culturetopia, individuals are self-motivated by the pleasure of doing good work.

In Culturetopia, doing good work is itself a big part of the motivation and the reward. People derive great satisfaction simply from doing things well. They get further pleasure from being recognized and even more from being remembered. What do people get when their main reason for doing something is being afraid of the boss? Maybe a sense of relief when it's all over: when they retire from work.

People can never do their best work when they are motivated exclusively by thoughts of what will happen if they don't do it. Best work only comes from people who are really engaged with an activity, who like the act of doing it, and who enjoy the results.

The link between a company's culture and employee performance is direct, dramatic, and durable.

Get the working environment right and you will create an upward spiral of performance, motivation, and fantastic customer service.

Let's think about the way that many people think the performance cycle works. The company's managers motivate and direct the workers, so the workers do good work and the customers are happy. What is wrong with this picture? For one thing, company managers and supervisors can't be everywhere all the time, sitting beside every employee, being motivators, and providing direction. Even when company bosses make great-sounding motivational speeches, we know for sure it doesn't last long. Any strong urge to do things differently is soon swamped by the daily pressures of business as usual. Somehow, employees need to be self-motivating and self-directing, all of the time, and the conventional way of thinking of this doesn't give us any insight into what a company must actually do to generate great results.

While most people think of the role of company management as primarily motivating and directing the workforce, I am convinced that the most important thing that a company can do is to work to create a company culture that enables employees to motivate and direct themselves all or almost all of the time.

To do this, a company must *allow* this to happen. Let employees work in areas that interest and engage them. Let employees interact and collaborate in whatever ways are necessary for them to serve internal and external customers. Free employees of the nuisances of disruptive behavior, micro management, and bureaucracy. Allow employees to exercise creativity and leadership and reward them whenever it pays off.

When the motivation to do good work comes from within each and every employee, we have a culture that enables high performance and is self-sustaining.

In Culturetopia, everyone has freedom.

The culture of accountability and responsibility has an impact on power and authority in the organization. What happens if we allow that kind of thinking to take over the organization?

Taking responsibility is the same as taking power. Accepting accountability ensures that the power is not misused. Mentors are there primarily to help create an environment in which these things can happen, not to police or micro manage.

This all adds up to more freedom for everyone. A company is not, and most will likely never be, a completely egalitarian, libertarian organism. But it can be a stimulating and pleasant place to work and a highly productive company at the same time. When people have a sense of being free, they flourish and will reward the company in turn.

In Culturetopia, everyone is:

- free to seize responsibility

- free to do good work

- free to make a creative and innovative contribution

- free from stress and anxiety

In Culturetopia, it is freedom that makes it worthwhile for people to come to work, and freedom that makes Culturetopian companies prosper.

13
The Culturetopia Values Checklist

Cultural strengths lead to high performance and success. Cultural weaknesses lead to poor performance.

As we have seen, there are a number of positive indicators of a *good* company culture, a culture that creates an environment in which employees can do their best work and where customers are nurtured and become loyal. By building these cultural strengths, a leadership team can orient the company for success.

You can use the checklist in this chapter to get a quick and rough assessment of your company's values and cultural environment. For a more rigorous assessment, you'll need to survey multiple people in your company and use a more detailed and finely grained assessment tool, but the checklist will get you started thinking about how your company shapes up. How close are you to Culturetopia?

For each one of the indicators listed below, simply assess whether each statement is true or false, or somewhere in the middle, for your company. Score the overall headings as well as the individual bullet points, giving you 35 line items in all. If you're not quite sure how to answer, go back to the relevant section earlier in the book. This time, think carefully about your own company as you read the description of the way things are in Culturetopia.

Decide where your organization stands and check the box if the statement is always or mostly *true*; leave the box empty if the statement is always or mostly *not true*, or if you don't know, or somewhere vague in between.

The Culturetopia Values Checklist

Values Drive the Business

☐ Values are built into the company's way of doing business.

☐ There are no conflicts in the application of values: there is complete and consistent values alignment.

There is a Shared Sense of Direction and Purpose

☐ Everyone knows why the company is in business.

☐ Everyone understands their individual role and how it contributes to the company's mission.

☐ Everyone acts in ways consistent with the company mission, always.

☐ There are standards, and everyone pays attention to them.

Customers Define the Approach to Business

☐ Everyone understands that customers pay for everything.

☐ Everyone has customers, and is a customer.

☐ The constant aim of everyone is to establish and maintain a positive and mutually beneficial relationship with all customers.

Mentors (Managers and Supervisors) are There to Help

☐ Mentors (managers and supervisors) exist primarily to increase job satisfaction in the workforce.

☐ The constant aim of management is to free employees to focus on the task.

☐ There is no disruptive behavior (and no one misses it).

☐ Frontline employees have the tools, materials, and space to do their jobs well.

☐ Mentors (managers and supervisors) always set a good example.

☐ Mentors (managers and supervisors) are expected to recruit people who are more talented than themselves.

Everyone is a Leader

☐ Everyone contributes through influencing and innovation.

☐ People hold themselves accountable and seize personal responsibility.

People Build Sound Relationships and High-Achieving Teams

☐ Relationships between individuals form the foundation of business success.

☐ Effective teams are recognized and nurtured as a source of motivation, productivity, creativity, and valuable innovation.

Everyone has Opportunities for Growth and Learning

☐ Mistakes and failures are used as opportunities for everyone to learn how to do things better.

☐ People are able to focus on doing the type of work they do best.

☐ Employees receive the coaching, training, and encouragement they need to do their best work.

Work is Satisfying and Rewarding for Everyone

☐ People are rewarded for producing results.

☐ Employees enjoy the working environment.

☐ Everyone feels that their everyday work is worthwhile: it's not a waste of their time or their lives.

☐ Individuals are self-motivated by the pleasure of doing good work.

☐ Everyone has freedom.

* * *

How does your organization rate?

You should have made a decision on each one of the 35 items above, checking just the boxes against the statements you consider to be always or mostly true.

Now, count the number of boxes you have checked.

29-35 Your company should be one of our case studies for how to do it right. Your company is a great place to work and there's a high probability that the company is financially successful.

22-28   Many successful companies are in this band. Your company has the potential to do much better, and already has a foundation for creating an even higher-performing culture.

15-21   Your company is middle-of-the-road. You get some things right, some things wrong. This is the type of company that often has not much sense of direction and most people probably find their personal satisfactions outside the company, not inside it. The good news? Lots of room for improvement.

8-14   Even more room for improvement here. Your company is likely in a downward spiral towards the lowest band.

0-7   Your company is probably a frustrating place to work, with lots of employee churn, and there's a high probability that the company is not financially successful. Changing course will not be easy because the pre-culturetopian habits are deeply ingrained.

* * *

What to do Next?

Congratulations on completing the survey! Whatever your score, at least you know more now than you did when you started. If this was a visit to the doctor's office, you've reached the point where you've replied to the question: "How are you today?" In other words, you've just started the process of diagnostics and treatment.

Remember that this survey is just a preliminary indicator. A more detailed analysis will be needed before you start to take action.

Meanwhile, the next step could be to get a small group of your work colleagues to go through the same assessment of your company. Do it independently at first, so you each capture your own perspectives. Then, one of you can consolidate the results on a spreadsheet: add up the total *Yes* scores for each item from all the people who responded. This will give you a numerical score for each item. Find some time to get together to compare perspectives.

Here are some suggestions to get the conversation going:

- Which item was given the highest score according to the group total? Discuss why the company does comparatively well in that area.

- Which item was given the lowest score by the group? Discuss why the company does not do so well in that area.

- Are there big differences in how the members of your group assigned scores? Does any one person disagree strongly with the others? Why is that?

- Look at the two or three items that received the worst group score. Discuss what might be the root cause(s) of these low scores.

- List some things the company can do to quickly address at least one of these underlying problems. What do you think is stopping the company from doing it?

- What are you going to do about it?

* * *

At this stage, some readers might be in a state of panic. Please don't despair: there *is* hope. Well, there might be hope. It is always possible to turn a team or small department around, no matter how bad the situation. But sustaining the change may be really hard work if the company itself is not clued in to the importance of culture in driving performance.

Turning a whole company around is more of a challenge, but it can be done, given the will and the right attitude at the top of the company.

If this checklist causes you to be concerned, then you should arrange for a more formal assessment, involving enough of your company employees to provide more substantial data for analysis. Visit our Web site at www.culturetopia.com for more information on how to go about this.

14
Aloha

———

Aloha is a wonderful Hawaiian word that is used, according to context, for hello or good-bye, or as an expression of love, affection, or compassion.

Aloha comes from two Hawaiian words: *alo*, meaning face or front or presence; and *ha*, meaning *breath of life*. Traditionally, when one Hawaiian met another, they would put their faces close together, say *alo* and then expel their breath in an emphatic *ha*. In this way, they would exchange the *breath of life* and symbolically share the *spirit of Aloha*.

Aloha has evolved to be much more than a greeting. Aloha has come to describe a spirit of sharing, cooperation, respect, and care for others, even when times are hard.

Does the ancient spirit of Aloha say anything to us, endeavoring to grow companies, creating positive work environments, and thriving in our jobs in the early 21st century? I believe so. As a frontliner, as a trainer, as a mentor, and as a consultant, I have grown to understand more clearly what makes people fulfilled with their lives. I have observed the different and complementary roles that competition and collaboration play in our national culture and in various corporate cultures, and I have gradually identified the common cultural characteristics of successful companies, as described in this book. During this time, I have warmed to Aloha, because the spirit of Aloha, or something like it, underpins the culture of many successful companies.

People need a purpose, a sense of accomplishing something worthwhile, to be really fulfilled in their lives. This quest for achievement is a primary driver of innovation, creativity, persistence, and hard work.

Competition provides a yardstick that can enhance the sense of achievement that comes from doing something well, and can also provide a stimulus to action. Competition has its place, but in many activities, it is effective collaboration and cooperation that really delivers great results. Successful individuals are never flying solo; they all depend on the willing support and collaboration of other people. Now and again, a unique talent does emerge, but even special people perform better when they work with a great team.

Leaders in Culturetopian companies have a sense of belonging to something bigger than themselves. These Culture Leaders encourage high performing teams that support, stimulate, and moderate each other. They care about the mission and they are motivated, determined, disciplined and unselfish.

Smart leaders get Aloha.

Smart leaders understand the importance of building a true performance culture where everyone can do their best work. They know when people achieve success it leads to lasting fulfillment for everyone. Smart leaders set their sights on moving their company closer to Culturetopia.

Aloha.

Further Reading

Buckingham, Marcus and Coffman, Curt
First Break All the Rules, Simon & Schuster, 1999.

Buckingham, Marcus and Clifton, Don
Now, Discover Your Strengths, Free Press, 2001.

Clifton, Don and Nelson, Paula
Soar With Your Strengths, Dell Books, 2nd edition, 1996.

Deal, Terrence and Kennedy, Alan
Corporate Cultures, Perseus, 1982.

Drucker, Peter F.
The Essential Drucker, HarperCollins, 2001.

Ericsson, K. Anders (ed.)
The Road to Excellence, Lawrence Erlbaum Associates, 1996.

Freiberg, Kevin and Freiberg, Jackie
Nuts!, Bard Press, 1996.

Fritz, Robert
Path of Least Resistance, Butterworth-Heinemann, 1994.

Gilbert, Daniel
Stumbling on Happiness, Knopf, 2006.

Gittell, Jody Hoffer
The Southwest Airlines Way, McGraw-Hill, 2003.

Goleman, Daniel
Emotional Intelligence, Bantam, 1995 (10th ed., 2005).

Haidt, Jonathon
The Happiness Hypothesis, Basic Books, 2006.

Kotter, John and Heskett, James
Corporate Culture and Performance, Simon & Schuster, 1992.

Rath, Tom and Clifton, Donald O.
How Full Is Your Bucket? Gallup Press, 2004.

Schein, Edgar H.
The Corporate Culture Survival Guide, Jossey-Bass, 1999.

Schein, Edgar H.
Organizational Culture and Leadership, Jossey-Bass, 1985 (3rd ed., 2004).

Schwartz, Barry
The Paradox of Choice, HarperCollins, 2004.

Seligman, Martin
Authentic Happiness, Free Press, 2002.

About the Author

Jason Young has been called a rare breed when it comes to developing leaders and customer service initiatives. As a former senior-level manager at Southwest Airlines Co., Jason learned the value of a successful workplace culture. During his 10-years with the airline consistently rated No. 1 in customer service and employee satisfaction, he was a key driver in creating and developing the company's innovative training programs for its successful leadership and customer service culture that have become renowned in the business world today.

Driven by the need to extend his unique insight in leadership development to others outside Southwest, Jason launched his own consulting practice to focus on corporate training and development services specializing in leadership, customer service and team building. Today, as president of LeadSmart, Inc., Jason shares his vision in developing successful corporate cultures and workplace environments with forward-thinking companies.

Capturing the innovative strategies and tactics he developed working with many Fortune 500 companies, Jason offers insights and practical information that can be implemented immediately in any organization. His keynote presentations and training programs are in demand for audiences of all types – from senior level executives to front line employees. Jason's messages reach to the core of every audience member with his unique style and engaging presentation skills. Participants are treated to a compelling experience that will change the way they view themselves, their customers and the company for which they work.

More info on Jason Young: **www.jasonyoungspeaks.com**

The most important step in training is the first one.

Measure first.

The first step in planning for your employee training and development needs is a clear understanding of the underlying issues in the organization. The key to an effective analysis is asking the right questions of the right people. An effective assessment tool must be able to survey individuals, teams or organizations with the right questions.

Culturetopia Culture Score is a powerful survey tool that measures the current cultural condition of any organization by asking critical questions around behaviors, attitudes and perspectives of every employee.

 Culturetopia Culture Score focuses on the distinctive values as outlined in *Cutluretopia* and provides a clear picture of the needs of a team or organization. Designed for a few or thousands of employees, Culturetopia Culture Score focuses on leadership practices, culture variables and specific behavior patterns that drive the important metrics of any organization. You'll walk away with a clear understanding and a benchmark of the foundational development needs of your organization.

More info at:
www.CultureScore.com